# UN
# REASON
Renegade
thinking for
leaders to create
impossible
change
# ABLE
# AMBITION

## VANESSA VERSHAW

I have seen first-hand the passion and drive Vanessa brings to every project, opportunity and coaching engagement. Her unwavering commitment to her own personal growth and development has inspired so many, myself included. Vanessa's move from North America to Australia was a loss to leaders in this country, but a big win for business thinking in Australia.

This book offers valuable lessons and insights that will help you clarify your aspirations, set ambitious targets and stay focused. It's a treasured resource for anyone seeking to make their dreams a reality.

**– Jeff Melanson, Partner, Stratagem and Unity Technologies, Jury member, Cannes Film Festival**

Vanessa Vershaw helps leaders understand the inner fears and barriers that are holding them back from being the best they can be. When her energy and curiosity for exploring peoples' ultimate potential is applied to entire leadership teams, the results are truly outstanding. Everyone touched by Vanessa through her work is ultimately better for the experience.

**– Kevin Gallagher, CEO, Santos**

Vanessa Vershaw is a true inspiration; her energy infuses all those around her. She's like adding truffle to your olive oil, taking your leadership to an entirely new level. Vanessa took me on a journey to level up my thinking and showed me that a world can exist beyond the one society chooses for you. I am forever transformed because of having her in my corner.

**– Dino Otranto, COO, Fortescue Metals Group**

Vanessa dares you to lead differently. Her work celebrates the unique skills of every individual, but ultimately manifests itself in a more positive mindset, more deeply engrained organisational values, greater cohesion and higher performance.

**– Chris Rodwell, CEO, Chamber of Commerce and Industry of Western Australia**

Vanessa's gift is her ability to help individuals and organisations flourish. Her success is built on her ability to win and hold trust. She provokes and guides positive change. She has inspired me to be true to my soul. She is the 'voice inside your head' that helps build leadership clarity, confidence, resilience and purpose.

**– Stephen Quantrill, Chairman and Non-Executive Director, McCrae Investments**

I have witnessed firsthand the long-lasting positive impact Vanessa has on those she works with. Under her skilled guidance she has helped us unlock our key people's potential and improved the culture of our business. Her guidance also helped our team to successfully navigate difficult post-GFC market conditions as she supported us through a period of significant growth.

**– Frank Cooper AO, Chairman and Non-Executive Director, Woodside Petroleum, South32, St John of God Health Care and the Insurance Commission of Western Australia**

Vanessa combines her extensive experience with an infectious energy that is rare to find in people. She can challenge and drive you to be the best version of yourself. Her empathy and love for people shines through in everything she does.

**– David Fyfe, CEO, Synergy**

Vanessa has had a long-lasting and very positive impact on Arc Infrastructure leading to a significant increase in individual and team performance, and the business's bottom line. Vanessa's style and energy make her a wonderful human being to spend time with.

**– Paul Larsen, former CEO, Arc Infrastructure; Non-Executive Chairman and Director, Perron Group, Centurion Transport and Kimberley Ports**

Vanessa has a differentiating and rare talent of creating breakthrough learning experiences for leaders, teams and organisations, generating the energy necessary for true and sustainable transformation.

**– Pat Reed, former Executive Manager, Walt Disney Corporation; Adjunct Professor, University of California, Berkeley**

Vanessa is an intellectually smart and savvy professional who understands that for businesses and people to survive and thrive in our ever-changing landscape they need tools beyond hard skills. We have forged an enduring partnership centred around our love of seeing organisations realise their unreasonable ambitions to become gamechangers. With Vanessa, anything is possible!

**– Fabian Ross, CEO, Hockey WA**

Vanessa was the catalyst to send me on my journey of self-confidence and growth and I haven't looked back. She helped me see myself for who I am – the strengths I never knew I had, and the weaknesses I didn't know how to tackle.

**– Mriganka Jaipuriyar, Head of News, Asia, S&P Global Platts**

Vanessa's style is infectious. She took me on a journey of discovery about myself, without which my career would not have reached the heights it has. Even through tough economic downturns I have maintained our work with Vanessa, recognising the massive value she brings to individuals and ultimately our organisation. Put simply, Vanessa gets it.

**– David Lewis, Managing Partner Tax – Energy, Utilities and Resources, PricewaterhouseCoopers London**

If you ever lose the key to yourself, Vanessa will unlock you to help you discover your true potential. With the power of positive reinforcement and unstinting belief, Vanessa is an extraordinary coach who released my true potential and enabled me to turbocharge my career aspirations.

**– Colin Campbell, Sales Director, ANZ, Adobe**

Vanessa has been an influencer in my own success and a much-appreciated confidant, always challenging for deeper thought and pushing the creative boundaries. Her insight, counsel and guidance has not only been valuable, it's been a core pillar of enabling business change and improvement. *Unreasonable Ambition* is a treasure trove of Vanessa's rich experiences which will leave readers reaching for more of that wisdom.

**– Andrew Broad, mining executive and CEO**

Vanessa Vershaw is a fireball of energy, enthusiasm and expertise. She is without peer when it comes to helping individuals and businesses to remove barriers, induce capability, plan actions and fast track ambitions. Her laser-sharp personal insight means that she is able to assist her clients to shine an ultra-bright spotlight on what matters most when pursuing goals of personal or strategic significance.

**– Emeritus Professor Gary Martin, CEO, Australian Institute of Management WA**

Vanessa has been a steadfast companion on my brave journey to starting my own organisation after several decades in executive-level technology roles in international organisations. She helped me articulate and realise new directions for the next exciting phase of my working life. I am so grateful to have met her.

**– Hiroko Sakaguchi, global technology executive**

Vanessa Vershaw is a professional without rival in her field. Working with her and being inspired by her helped me to grow exponentially as a leader. She remains very important in my life today.

**– Raphaël Lapointe, banking and finance executive**

Working with Vanessa Vershaw over many years and numerous projects, she has always demonstrated laser-focused thinking and listening skills to get you to the crux of the issues quickly. She's a tough taskmaster who brings out your best thinking and holds you to your delivery commitments.

**– Kevin Brown, CEO, St John Ambulance**

'Come to the edge,' he said.
'We can't, we're afraid!' they responded.
'Come to the edge,' he said.
'We can't, we will fall!' they responded.
'Come to the edge,' he said.
And so they came.
And he pushed them.
And they flew.

– Guillaume Apollinaire

**Disclaimer**

# CONTENTS

# UNREASONABLE AMBITION LEADERSHIP MANIFESTO

We are the **unreasonably ambitious**.

We face life with **confidence** and **courage**. We choose to go **beyond resilience**, pursuing success with **unreasonable ambition**.

Adventure seekers, we are attracted to the thrill of exploring **new frontiers** and **roads less travelled**, no matter how perilous, thinking big and beyond.

Energised by unreasonably ambitious agendas, we are first to **lead into the unknown**, making it safe for others to follow.

We live a life of **awe, wonder and limitless possibility**.
We're grateful for all the gifts we have been afforded.

Compelled to go against the grain, we revel in uncertainty, trusting in our ability to solve impossible challenges **against all odds**.

Rebels with a cause, we are driven by a higher calling to **make a difference** in our world.

We are **relentless** and **passionate** in our pursuits and boldly **inspire** others to action.

We are **humble** and copy no-one, leveraging our creativity to imagine worlds that don't exist yet for others to play in.

We believe in **magic** and **miracles**. We have unshakeable faith in the **limitless potential** of all people and our planet.

We don't run from the storm. We *are* the storm.

Available for download from www.vanessavershaw.com/manifesto

# PREFACE

*I believe in human potential. I believe that people have
the answers within them. As a coach, I seek to develop people
beyond the limits of their own knowledge.*

— Vanessa Vershaw

**I found him.
Curled up in the corner of his office,
rocking back and forth, sobbing.
A wreck.**

I still don't know how I ended up in the penthouse suite of a downtown skyscraper in Perth, Western Australia holding a middle-aged man crying in my arms. My life has always been like this: a series of serendipitous moments and encounters that have placed me at the epicentre of human trial and triumph.

That morning had started just like any other. The birds were chirping and the flowers were in full bloom on a gorgeous spring day. I was on my way to work with a well-known mining magnate at his ultra-sleek, well-designed office in the city. I really enjoyed going there; there is nothing quite like being in luxurious surrounds to make you feel successful and on top of your game. My energy was supercharged. The organisation was going through a sea change, and I had been engaged to help them transition into a reimagined future during a state of severe economic upheaval.

As context, the resources sector had just entered a bust phase and many companies were fighting to keep their doors open, which was causing panic throughout the business community. To put this into perspective, in Australia the resources sector (mining, oil and gas production) contributes around 10 per cent of GDP (US$150 billion), and about the same amount to export income, which amounts to around 50 per cent of exports.[1] So, there was no question that we were at a major fork in our economic road, and it wasn't looking great.

This wasn't just an Australia thing. Globally, we had entered a state of recession considered by many economists to have been the most serious financial crisis since the Great Depression. Most banks had been bailed out by government to avoid bankruptcy and millions of people had lost their jobs. Fortunately, we were not hit as hard in Australia compared with the rest of the world.

So, why was this man so distraught?

I consoled him and coached him 'off the ledge'. He had enjoyed years of abundance and profit without much effort as supreme market ruler. His arrogance had built a company culture of entitled jerks who had grown fat from greed. Their shaky relationships with customers could best be described as one-night stands. In a few months, he had gone from feeling like master of the universe to wondering whether the company would survive to trade another day. He was on his knees, and he didn't know how to get up.

The atmosphere was intense and heavy. Manic and surging. It was exhausting.

Later that afternoon, I visited another client just up the road. I still felt the weight of where I had been. I quickly noticed that the birds were still singing, and the skies were a magnificent powder-blue, cloudless, and stretched as far as the eyes could see. It was as if, outside of this bubble, time had stood still. I was reminded that life goes on, and so must we.

The next office was as impressive as the last. Yet, this time, I was met with very different energy.

There he was, another resources Titan standing up and looking out the window with a huge smile across his face. He welcomed me into his office with eager anticipation, walking over to open the door to let me in (what a gentleman!). He was bursting at the seams with excitement. He had built the prototype of a new technology product that was set to revolutionise the mining sector. If all went to plan, he would create a new market space. His vision was that mining companies were no longer going to be operating purely in the business of mining; they were going to be technology businesses. Mr Titan was a force to be reckoned with – you could feel it!

In truth, while I was delighted to be met with such enthusiasm, it also felt mentally jarring after spending the morning with the other man – Mr Magnate, who felt his empire was crumbling around him.

Why was this man so happy? The world was supposedly blowing up and this guy was smiling, ready to step into battle and take on the war.

How is it that two people going through similar experiences could respond so differently? Both men would be considered clever, famous and wealthy beyond measure. From the outside looking in, they ticked all the boxes in terms of the popular definitions of success. But there was actually a huge difference between them. One that, at the end of the day, would result in a winner who would keep winning and a loser who would be left behind.

\*

After two decades' work in helping leaders shift their mindset to be resilient and adaptive to change, I have realised that a clear difference exists between those who thrive on the edge of the precipice and those who fall into the abyss. In the areas of psychology and human performance, there are distinct qualities, characteristics and ways of working that separate people's success levels and life enjoyment.

And it's this: unreasonable ambition.

I believe ambition to be the most primal and sacred foundation of our human essence. To feel ambition and act upon it is the calling of our souls. It's a deep stirring that when acted upon puts us on our unique life path. To resist the inner calling is to risk living a life that is less than we are capable of, and to deny ourselves the gift of living our best lives. Being ambitious is to be *driven by a higher calling*. I describe it as having a raging fire in your belly that fuels you to overcome fear, doubt and resistance and drives you to action.

Perhaps you know this feeling?

**Being ambitious is to be driven by a higher calling. I describe it as having a raging fire in your belly that fuels you to overcome fear, doubt and resistance and drives you to action.**

Mr Titan was living an ambitious and inspired life. He was focused on leading from the edge to realise his craziest dreams, and taking everyone along with him. He was energised by adversity; the loftier the challenge, the more driven he became to succeed.

Mr Magnate, on the other hand, had become a victim to his own self-limiting beliefs. Immobilised by fear and a need for control, he had low expectations, set goals below his capacity and had limited his potential for ingenuity and growth. He was on a fast track to mediocrity.

But being ambitious is not enough. Great leaders must also be unreasonable.

Think about William the Conqueror, one of the greatest kings in history. William was ambitious, yes, but he would never have led the Norman invasion of England and became the last foreign conqueror of the country if he had been reasonable. He set unreasonable goals that set his sights beyond British shores. And, let's face it, William the Reasonable doesn't have quite the same ring to it, does it?

Being unreasonable is about having a pioneering world view. It's about renegade thinking for big and beyond.

Here is the simple truth. The secret to leading today for a successful tomorrow can be reduced to three principles:

1. To be *ambitious* is survival.
2. To be *reasonable* is dangerous.
3. To be *unreasonable* is necessary.

By the end of this book, you will have everything you need to access the greatness inside you that is waiting to be unleashed onto the world. It's then that you can step into your full potential and lead a life of unreasonable ambition.

— *Vanessa Vershaw*

# INTRODUCTION: YOU WERE BORN FOR THIS

*The difference between what we do and what we are capable of doing would suffice to solve most of the world's problems.*

– Mahatma Gandhi

We are in a catalytic era. A tornado of change has descended and humanity is caught in the maelstrom. Business leaders are facing an unknown future trying to figure out how to navigate the way, armed only with an outdated roadmap, bad intel and obsolete operating systems.

Wherever we are, we are witnessing extreme reactions at both ends of the spectrum. Some leaders are energised by the adventure of what lies ahead. Others are straining under the burden of confronting a future that is largely unchartered, with no rulebook or guardrails. The only way to step into the future as it emerges is to create the future for ourselves.

You'd agree that this is not a time to be reasonable.

Circumstance has given us carte blanche to reimagine the world we want to live in. But to bend the world to our vision for a brighter future, we must have unreasonable ambitions for what's possible. We must hold relentless optimism about the prospect of changing the world, and confront brutal realism about the obstacles to doing so.

---

**We must hold relentless optimism about the prospect of changing the world, and confront brutal realism about the obstacles to doing so.**

---

Your ability to flourish in an ever-morphing world will be fuelled by:

· the drive of your higher ambitions
· your preparedness to set unreasonable goals
· your willingness to believe that you are capable of far more than you believe
· your ability to unearth the greatness you were born with to achieve the impossible.

It is time to stop running from the storm.

It is time to *be the storm* and become the entrepreneur of your own life.

## FINDING YOUR UNREASONABLE AMBITION

Whether you believe it or not, everyone was born unreasonable and has some kind of hero inside them.

I should know.

There are so many days when I sit quietly in my office, pinching myself and asking myself the question, 'How did I end up here?'

How did I become a leadership coach to ASX-20 and Fortune 100 companies? When did I become the trusted advisor, coaching and mentoring some of the world's most well-known movers and shakers in every industry – from toilet-paper manufacturing to investment banking, from oil wells to railways, from entertainment to technology?

How is it that an ordinary person like me can go into a room with people who are far more well known and successful than I am, and be invited into their worlds as a guide on their journey through life? (I am asked this often.) That evolution story is part of my becoming.

I have realised that I was born with a mindset of unreasonable ambition. And the truth is, the *how* of my being and doing is not something I have consciously thought about – until now.

I was inspired to write *Unreasonable Ambition* because I have learned from personal experience what it takes to transcend the opaque barriers of challenging life circumstances and shaky self-belief to create an amazing life. Some might say I have seen it all (well, maybe not all – people do still surprise me sometimes!).

If you met me in person, you would never know I had survived the darkest of moments – childhood trauma and abuse, and a parent battling addiction. I don't wear the 'abused' tag branded on my forehead. There are no visible signs of my emotional wounds and scars.

To the contrary: I'm poised, polished and present well (I'm a target for the insecure!). I'm a well-travelled global citizen. I walk with pride, determination and a skip in my step.

I'm an enigma to those who don't know me well.

The more likely fate for someone who has survived abuse and experienced the rollercoaster ride of financial highs and lows is a radically different life to what I've created. Research tells me I could very easily have ended up on the street, battling my own drug habit. Like many women with a background like mine, I could have found myself peddling my sex to make a few bucks or tagged as some Jane Doe in the morgue with no-one to claim me. Dead and forgotten.

But by multiple strokes of good fortune, hard work and perhaps a sprinkle of fairy dust that's not how I ended up.

I am still here. Alive and kicking. Doing what I love. Working with incredible people. Surrounded by a supportive community. Leading others with passion, ferocious intent and unreasonable ambition.

I have silenced old records to rise above a past that does not define me.

And here is what I put it down to.

I was born with a fire blazing within, a hungry mind roaring to question and a soul impatient to evolve. I have always had the desire to create the world I want to live in, drawing on all parts of myself as dreamer, visionary, magician, leader and healer.

I became the entrepreneur of my life, creating it and shaping it with each step I have taken.

I am living proof that human success is not dictated by the stress and conditioning of life circumstances, but by how high we choose to rise – by having ambitions that are viewed as otherwise unreasonable. And by being able to execute them.

The reality is that right now we are all being tested. The stress that comes from trying to keep pace with change, make sense of a future we cannot fathom and rely more greatly on intuition is terrifying.

It's turning many into the worst version of themselves: heads spinning, struggling to keep up with the pace of change. On a broader scale it's manifesting as rising mental health concerns, physical illness and a society that is disconnected, plastic and lost.

But what if I told you that you too are hardwired to be unreasonably ambitious? That you have the capacity to turn your anxiety into exhilaration and your fears into courage that you had forgotten you have?

You are exponentially more capable of leveraging more internal resources than you do right now. Within you lies the ability to accelerate your learning by 200 per cent, and your creativity by 400 per cent.

What difference would that make to your life? To realise your wildest dreams beyond measure?

**I am living proof that human success is not dictated by the stress and conditioning of life circumstances, but by how high we choose to rise.**

I believe that everyone has a sleeping giant within them. The challenge is knowing how to wake it up. The secret lies in breaking through our mental barriers into our untapped reservoir of potential – that extra 60 per cent that lies dormant and underutilised.

It's about finding the key to unlocking what is already within you. The price of admission to unlocking your full potential is to open your mind, do some heavy lifting to outsmart your biology, lean into your instincts and believe before you see.

And then it's about making it happen.

## GETTING THE MOST OUT OF THIS BOOK

*It's never too late to be who you might have been.*
– George Eliot

I am someone who like things organised, grounded, simple and clean. Anyone who works with me will tell you that I cut to the chase and keep it real (whether they like it or not!).

So here it is. There are loads of books out there that provide great thought leadership about how to build the mindset and skillset to tap into your innate stores of unreasonable ambition, natural agility and resilience.

But here's the thing: it's easy to say 'go and develop unreasonable ambition' or 'go and build your resilience', but these states of being are difficult to define and even harder to achieve. Yet, there are specific ways of thinking, being and doing that will power your bounce-back; simple ways to hack your hardwiring, fast.

I'm a big believer in using real words, not big words, so that you get the most out of this book. No psychobabble or consultant-speak in here. I promise.

I am committed to demystifying things for you and challenging prevailing myths about what it takes to achieve success in life and at work. In this book you will find the golden ticket to a meaningful and exciting life where *you* call the shots.

I'll be sharing my 20 years of global experience and psychological techniques to prepare you for your best life. I'll be showcasing the inside stories of some of the most unreasonably ambitious leaders I have been privileged to spend time with – the shooting stars, the unsung heroes and the angels among us, weaving their threads through our lives without fanfare and yet deserving of our utmost gratitude.

These are extraordinary humans, and many have come from nothing. They're ordinary folk from everyday – sometimes impoverished – beginnings who have transcended their designated station to achieve amazing things, jump s-curves and build empires without supernatural powers or the support of a genie in a bottle. They've made full use of their gifts and talents to lead a purpose-driven life.

It's all about futures that know no boundaries. Happy lives fulfilled. Legacies that are built to last.

The book is divided into four parts:

I.   Motivation
II.  Mantra
III. Mindset
IV.  Momentum.

Any great adventure starts with *motivation* – the fire in your belly that compels you to care. So many leaders I have worked with describe motivation as an overwhelming urge to take action that forces them to make a change. Understanding your new operating context and being driven by a greater purpose is what we will be uncovering in part I. To make unique contributions that have big impact you need to understand what the world needs from you and what unreasonable ambition looks like in practice – the good, the bad and the ugly.

Then, in part II, it's about setting your *mantra*. This is your commitment to being the best version of yourself – knowing who you are and keeping it real. We'll look at the power of self-awareness, and how to tap into your bigger life purpose and invest in your future self to set up a blueprint for the work and home life you crave. This will give you clarity around where to direct your intentions and your efforts.

Part III is where the rubber hits the road. Pruning, cultivating and growing an unreasonably ambitious *mindset* is the secret to sustained happiness and high performance. I am going to take you through eight adaptive challenges to elevate your gifts and support you in leading your life with courage, clear intention and absolute focus. Think of these as mind hacks to accelerate your ability to jump from darkness to possibility. Part III is not for the faint-hearted. It will stretch your mind and provide a pathway for you to accelerate your leadership impact at work and at home.

The book concludes with part IV – *momentum*. Being able to reinforce and sustain all that you have learned requires deliberate practice and adaptive action. I will do a wrap-up of everything we have learned and prepare you for what's to come.

By the end of *Unreasonable Ambition*, you may feel a bit jibbed. You may ask yourself the question, 'How come no-one has told me this before?'

And then you will know. You are forever altered – seeing the world with fresh eyes. You're ready to be more. Create more. Do more.

Not everyone has crazy life dreams and ambitions to make a dent in the universe. Not everyone wants to be a changemaker, a rainmaker or a modern-day revolutionary. But if you're one of those who does, it's time to clear the path to blaze your trail and lead the world better.

It's time to stop running from the storm and *become* the storm.

So here is my invitation to you as we begin our intrepid journey together. I invite you to drop the anchor on old stories on repeat.

I implore you to turn your back on a past that does not define you.

I encourage you to stay open and curious.

I ask you to trust your intuition.

I dare you to lead with unreasonable ambition to create your own future.

I urge you to take the road less travelled, and become the leader were born to be.

So, what are you waiting for? Let's get started.

# PART I

# MOTIV ATION

Ambition is the path to success.
Persistence is the vehicle you arrive in.

– BILL BRADLEY

One of the most confronting experiences I have ever had was while doing my psychologist training at a local hospital in Western Australia. I had been placed on the children's ward in the psychology unit. The ward was divided up into two key areas – one for the kids with relatively common mental health challenges, and the other for the more complex cases.

It was early morning, and as I strolled down the corridor I peeked into the 'cells', curious to see what the children were doing stuck in their rooms all day. I had never been to a facility like this before and I was feeling quite anxious about it. My deep empathy for children tended to override my ability to keep clinical distance. That's a no-no for psychologists, by the way. Not being able to separate personal feelings from your professional work makes it almost impossible to make decisions for prescribed treatments unclouded by emotions.

As an empath this has always been an ongoing challenge (it's how I ended up becoming an organisational psychologist after coming to terms with my limits!). Being an empath means that I'm highly intuitive. I can easily feel others' emotions. It sounds super intense, I know – but I have quickly become accustomed to it, and the benefits that go with it (so have my clients!). With this gift comes the power of knowing others – being able to tune into others at a higher frequency to sense their thoughts, innermost fears and desires. So, you can understand why I resisted the placement at first. A children's mental health hospital is not usually a welcomed place for an energy sponge like me.

A loud banging sound accompanied by desperate wailing stopped me in my tracks. I looked in through the window to see a little boy, about nine years old, dressed in his pyjamas and repeatedly banging his head against the wall. I noticed that his poor little head was a deep purple, covered in bruises, contusions and perspiration. He was so distressed. Yet, despite the pain he was inflicting on himself he continued to bang his head against the wall, repeatedly, until it bled.

As confronting as the scene was, in that moment I became a better psychologist. I believe that sometimes the worst experiences can spark the greatest insights, and this was one of those times.

Here's what I learned: that there is often tension between what is good for us and what we want to do.

The little boy was compelled to relieve the pain of his suffering by banging his head against the wall. He chose to inflict himself with physical pain to help manage his psychological anguish. He chose the lesser of two evils to cope with his situation.

Here's the problem: as human beings we are creatures of habit. Our preference is usually to stick with what we know, play it safe and live inside the bubbles of our own creation without venturing out – even if it is bad for us.

It's why people stay in toxic relationships. It's why losing weight can be so hard. It's why leaders fail to step up to the plate and lead their organisations into an unknown future.

It's why the little boy continued to bang his head, no matter how much it hurt him.

Our brains trick us into staying the same. They think they're doing us a favour, protecting us from harm.

But they're not. They're preventing us from being able to generate the motivation and focus we need to push through the obstacles, climb the mountains and move in our desired direction.

Let's consider weight loss for a second. How often have you heard someone say they can't exercise because they are too tired after a long day at work? But the fatigue they are experiencing is not physical. They have been sitting on their butts all day! What they are actually experiencing is *mental fatigue*.

Let's face it, we have all been prey to responding to false signals from the brain telling us to stay sedentary, passive and inactive. It's our mind's way of protecting us to maintain homeostasis and settle into a comfortable state of steady functioning. To keep us exactly as we are; not growing, not evolving.

But here's the thing: if you can push past this false survivor state and start exercising, something amazing happens. You'll experience the most satisfying workout of your life. Energy will start to rush through your body. (And you'll be thanking me for getting you out of your chair!)

Keeping your brain in great shape, creating new habits and becoming revitalised needs a lot of motivation and surplus energy. That's why part I of the book is dedicated to helping you get motivated. It's about finding your greater purpose; your reason to get up in the morning even when you may not feel like it. Finding the urgency to care and act, no matter what life is throwing at you, no matter how painful or frightening the situation.

Every person with unreasonable ambition is driven by an unearthly rumbling to succeed; fuelled by the desire to be more; propelled by an insatiable hunger to create change in the world.

---

**Every person *with unreasonable ambition* is driven by an unearthly rumbling to succeed.**

---

There's science behind being able to generate the energy you need to push yourself forward and block out the noise that makes you want to bang your head against a brick wall. But first, we will work to understand the role of motivation in helping you bust through ingrained habits to get to your bigger *why*. It starts with understanding what the world looks like around you, the size of the challenge the future is setting for you and how you need to respond.

We will also delve deeper into profiling what an unreasonably ambitious leader looks like in the flesh – warts and all – so you can set some personal goals.

Life is goading you with an extreme adaptive challenge to activate the unreasonable ambition that is already in you. So, buckle up and brace yourself. Answer a higher call and deliver what the world needs from you right now – no matter how wild the ride.

It's time to fire up your full potential!

# CHAPTER 1

# THE WORLD HAS CHANGED

The future doesn't care how you became an expert.

– DAVID BLAKE

Like the shifting of tectonic plates on the earth's surface, we have moved into an era of seismic paradigm change. We're floating in and out of liminal spaces,[2] caught between two worlds where nothing is certain, nothing is clear and everything we thought was important is on hold.

The word 'liminal' comes from the Latin root *limen*, which means 'threshold'. The liminal space is the 'crossing over' space – the space where you have left something behind, yet you are not yet fully in the next thing. It's a transition space, an in-between space heralding transformative opportunity. It's a time to uncover moments of uncertainty that are also ripe with possibility.

## YOUR NEW OPERATING CONTEXT

Life is fast and furious. Our operating context has shifted at warp speed, going from VUCA (volatile, uncertain, complex and ambiguous) to TUNA (turbulent, uncertain, novel and ambiguous) almost overnight in the wake of a global pandemic that no-one really saw coming.

'Black swan' events such as Covid-19 and 'grey rhino' events such as Kodak going defunct and Blockbuster going bust have become commonplace in our daily grind.[3] Even occurrences such as the Great Resignation or Attrition (depending on your stance), where millions of people around the globe are quitting their jobs without necessarily having another job to go to, is part and parcel of the new world order (I'm not sure why employers are so baffled by it!). It's the domino effect of a race going through major disruption and upheaval – and it's not going to let up anytime soon.

---

**As a leader, your ability to move with the change will dictate the magnitude of your rise or fall.**

---

What is clear is this: as a leader, your ability to move with the change will dictate the magnitude of your rise or fall.

## HOW ARE YOU GETTING IN YOUR OWN WAY?

One of the biggest barriers to success is relying on known ways of thinking to solve life and business challenges. Yet that is what most of us are doing. Driven by fear, our craving for certainty and our need to feel in control sees us setting ourselves up to measure a successful past – rather than building the capability to get in front of the curve and read the signs of today.

Our current ways of doing business are set up for repeatable events and stable market conditions. The human mind is great at identifying patterns, creating short cuts (also known as schemas) and relying on historical data. So, when we are confronted by unknown challenges, our natural tendency is to identify trends we are already aware of.

This is *bad*.

Your standard operating procedures won't work in the face of the unlikely or improbable. They will fail you in situations that are new, or that you are dealing with for the first time. In *The Practice of Adaptive Leadership*, authors Ronald A Heifetz, Alexander Grashow and Marty Linsky state it well: 'The most common leadership failure stems from trying to apply technical solutions to adaptive challenges.'[4]

So, how do you short-circuit your neural programming to move faster through any type of change and become unreasonably ambitious?

## LEADERS CAN BE MADE

A recent study examined the mindsets, behaviours and skillsets of some of the world's most successful leaders, and it discovered something startling: you don't have to be born with the goods straight out of the womb.[5] *You can become a great leader.* You can develop unreasonable ambition.

And that's why this book is for everyone. You don't have to 'qualify' to read it.

As human beings we all have fears and doubts to overcome. But the difference between those who realise their unreasonable ambitions and those who don't is that the former don't let their fears and doubts stop them from taking action. They do it anyway! And that is what this book is about – *becoming*. Unearthing the unreasonably ambitious leader you already are.

It's a deliberate choice and it starts with powerful intention. Leaders with unreasonable ambition are compelled to think beyond the norms of conventional wisdom and logic. They question their default position to explore other options, and then they just get on with it.

Lauded organisational psychologist Adam Grant calls this 'vuja de', the opposite of 'deja vu'. It's when we face something familiar but see it with fresh perspective that enables us to gain new insights into old problems.[6] Let's take a look at what the research tells us about our natural leadership potential.

## THE 6 Cs

A research team set out to devise a winning formula to be a better modern-day leader. They investigated many of the world's most well-known, successful leaders, evaluating the creative ideas of Apple's Steve Jobs, the insights of the Dalai Lama, the business instincts of Amazon's Jeff Bezos, the endurance of ironman Trevor Hendy and the strategic mind of chess master Magnus Carlsen.

After analysing more than 1000 academic articles and mapping psychological, biological and brain patterns, the researchers came up with a list of six capabilities needed to succeed in this age of the Fourth Industrial Revolution.[7] These were capacity, choice, connection, collaboration, change agility and creativity.[8] They're illustrated below.

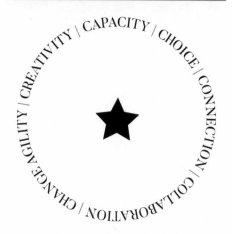

Six capabilities for success

Let's take a look at these in more detail:

- **Capacity** is about being resilient and maintaining a driving sense of purpose during tough times.

- **Choice** is an ability to operate with System 2 Thinking – the mind's slower analytical mode, where reason dominates. In contrast, System 1 Thinking is the brain's fast, automatic, intuitive response.

- **Connection** is about relating to others and demonstrating compassion. It was also found to have the highest correlation with productivity and profitability. This was linked to empathy, where the leader's ability to see the world through the lens of another has been deemed critical to internal and external customer engagement and maintaining a competitive edge.

- **Collaboration** is a skill critical to maintaining a performance edge. This requires leaders to move from centralised decision-making models to becoming coaches and facilitators of teams. It also supercharges their ability to learn and generate new knowledge fast.

- **Change agility** is the ability to resist non-value-adding processes, becoming hyperaware, making sense of external trends and high-velocity decision-making.

- **Creativity** is the ability to deliver nonlinear thinking and innovation. An entrepreneurial mindset is a key part of this superpower.

The 6 Cs research provides us with a solid foundation to explore the essence of unreasonable ambition in action. The findings also confirm that the potential to be more lies within all of us.

But the 6 Cs are not enough. They illustrate what is *sufficient* to maintain where you are right now, but *not* what will help you level up to *thrive* (I promise I will take you there shortly!).

\*

Before we continue our journey together, let's take a moment to summarise some key points.

To be an unreasonably ambitious leader is to face the stark truth of disruption today, knowing that if you don't own and drive your own evolution, you will quickly become irrelevant.

Our world – the way we live, the way we love, the way we connect, the way we work – has changed dramatically. Business models are developing faster than ever before, and leadership lessons such as these teach us that we must keep pace to survive and disrupt ourselves to create the lives our souls crave.

And so, as the world continues to rapidly morph, so must you!

To move with the storm, you must *be the storm*.

## Reflection

- How has the world changed for you? What is it demanding from you?

- What are the benefits of staying exactly as you are?

- How are old habits and ways of thinking getting in the way of your own progress?

# CHAPTER 2

# BE THE STORM

There is no shortage of causes in the world, just a shortage of leaders who can inspire us to pursue them.

– SIMON SINEK

We are all being tested.

No-one is immune to the forces that are transforming business and society. We are all trying to figure out how to adapt to the new logic of business competition, create opportunity from uncertainty and prepare to thrive in our lives and at work.

In this environment, it is the unreasonably ambitious leaders who are able to swim through the upheaval with stronger strokes and chart a course, while others are paralysed by fear, unable to dive off the starting blocks.

Your ability to create the life you want hinges on how fast you can lean into uncertainty and resist your natural urge to duck for cover or freeze like a deer in the headlights. It's about getting comfortable feeling completely out of your depth. If you don't, you risk being left behind.

## YOU HAVE BEEN HERE BEFORE

Everyone has a story – the story of how they came to be, of the highs and lows of their life's journey that sparked moments of extraordinary growth. Along the way are serendipitous events, milestone moments and other influential humans that changed the course of their life in an instant.

We have all gone through difficult times. Our bodies store these experiences as physiological imprints – especially when we experience trauma, or situations of extreme stress that cause the body to fight, flee or freeze to cope.

Think of your body as a map of every experience you have ever had, good and bad. Your body holds your memories tightly inside you.

To be able to let go of fear and build bravery we must access what we've already been through. We must tap into those moments when we triumphed; when we were strengthened by what occurred. Thirteenth-century Sufi poet Rumi said, 'The cure for the pain is in the pain.' There's wisdom in that.

**You are more ready than you think to tackle whatever comes your way.**

It's time to remember that you have been here before. You are more ready than you think to tackle whatever comes your way. To begin your quest means starting from exactly where you are right now.

## Reflection

· How has your past prepared you to lead better today?

· What are the internal resources that you have relied on most to bring you success so far?

## UNLEASHING YOUR INNER WARRIOR

There's a powerful and super-simple exercise I run with teams to try to access transformative memories. It's also a formidable way to demonstrate the power of collective strength.

On the lifeline illustrated in the figure below, I ask participants to plot their life as a series of positive and negative experiences in chronological order.

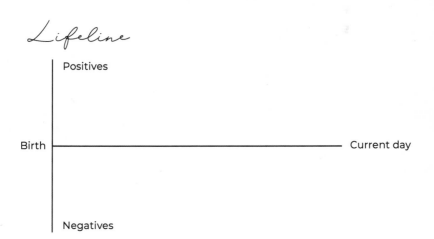

After they complete the exercise, I ask them to write down the leadership qualities they developed as a result of each experience on their timeline. The revelations are often mind-blowing. Two critical shifts occur.

The first is that people recognise that they have more internal resources and influence within them than they imagined. They are stronger, braver and better prepared for the future than they thought. This is usually a very emotional experience for people as they recall milestone events and significant people in their lives that have shaped them. I often see the powerful impact of teachers and mentors here.

The second shift is with the collective team, as people identify that together they have all the prerequisite capabilities needed to tackle whatever is coming their way. That they can merge as one and confront the future head-on. (Often we get so busy at work that we don't take the time to really get to know one another. When we do, it changes *everything*.)

I encourage you to do this exercise and see where you land.

## Reflection

· What did you learn about yourself and your own strength and capability through this exercise?

· If you did this with your team, how did it alter your perceptions of different team members?

Leading with unreasonable ambition also means recognising the limitations of our own individual giftedness and that the greater power comes from leveraging the brilliance of the collective.

Let me share with you the story about a man who removed the anchor of his past to create new beginnings. He re-wrote his own story to narrate a new one that was even better.

## THERE'S NO PLACE LIKE HOME

*At the end of the day, it isn't where I came from. Maybe home is somewhere I am going and never have been before.*

– Warsan Shire

I will never forget meeting Stephen Quantrill. Quantrill was a former banking and finance executive from Durban, South Africa. Our meeting was serendipitous to say the least. I had been scouted by one of his board directors to assist with the transformation of a low-performing manufacturing asset and prepare it for sale. I learned that Quantrill had held several high-level roles at Old Mutual Plc and Nedcor Bank Limited; at one stage, he even reported to South African-born Gail Kelly, well known in Australia as the former CEO of Westpac. After founding several business ventures that had mixed success, and still nursing wounds from a partnership gone sour, Quantrill went on to manage the private fortune of one of Australia's most lauded pioneers in engineering and construction: Harold Clough.

So just how did this quietly spoken South African native go from fleeing a country marked by violence and civil unrest to managing the millions of an Australian business icon?

One fine summer's day in 2013, on a golf course by the sea, Quantrill met one of Clough's family members who introduced him to their 'dad'. After a brief meeting where he formed instant synergy, he was offered an opportunity that became the role of a lifetime (it didn't happen overnight, but eventually materialised into his current role). Part of Quantrill's appeal is his low-key, affable style. He has a serene energy about him that creates a feeling of instant trust and safety. This is in addition to his amazing educational pedigree. (He's very well-rounded. He even shared with me he started to study Arts but ended up succumbing to taking a more 'pragmatic' study route. His life has been anything but.)

I'm wondering if you have guessed where I am leading you right now. Is the power of his story the fact that he scored a 'dream' job, or something more?

## LANDING IN THE WAITING SPACE

Quantrill's story has so many layers. It's a story of multiple life transitions; about moving from what has been to what will be. It's about dancing in perpetual ambiguity and trusting an unknown life path.

Quantrill journeyed from turbulence to safety; from home to a new frontier; from overconfidence to humility; from grit to tenacity; from cocoon to butterfly. He grew up in a stable middle-class family environment, his father a radiologist and his mother a supportive wife. He was the captain of his rugby team and continued to rise into leadership roles once he graduated from university. It was after getting married and the birth of his children that the increasing crime and unrest in South Africa started to play on his mind. He became increasingly worried about his family's safety. When his wife's life was put at risk, he made the decision to leave his beloved South Africa and travel to the distant shores of Western Australia.

Shaken loose from his foundation, Quantrill received an invitation to surrender to his potential, allowing his old self to dissolve to make way for something bigger. His unreasonably ambitious mindset enabled him to create a new future for himself, one new experience at a time, and reinvent himself in the process.

Quantrill's new life began when he let go of the need for certainty and stepped out of his comfort zone to greet an unknown future. In doing so, he jumpstarted his own metamorphosis.

As the saying goes, the magic happens outside our comfort zone. Transformation occurs when we are not in charge.

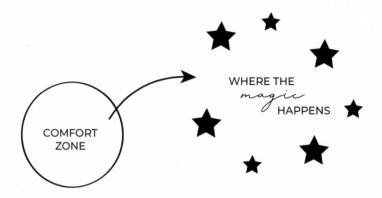

To become unreasonably ambitious, we must break out of the cocoon enveloping us in old ways of being, thinking and doing that no longer serve us. These cocoons, which represent safety and comfort, can imprison our potential if we don't let go of the fear and control to make way for our genius to rise.

---

**Transformation happens when we are not in charge.**

---

That's when the real magic happens. That's when the butterfly emerges.

Quantrill's story is a living example of an unreasonably ambitious leader who was prepared to disrupt himself by blowing up his old life to create a new one.

## Reflection

· Which gifts are gathering dust in your leadership toolkit?

· What are you prepared to 'blow up' to make room for opportunity to enter?

· What new story do you need to write for yourself?

# CHAPTER 3

# WHY THE WORLD NEEDS YOU

The reasonable man adapts himself to the world;
the unreasonable one persists in trying to adapt the world
to himself. Therefore, all progress depends on the
unreasonable man.

– GEORGE BERNARD SHAW[9]

When I was 12 years old, I had an experience that shook me to my core. I was attending mass at my local parish. I patiently sat in the pew listening to the sermon being delivered by Father Jack, an evangelical priest visiting from the US. Father Jack's voice was so loud it was deafening. For the audience of low-key Catholics, mostly families with small children or seniors over 60, his bombastic sermonising was offensive. He caused visible discomfort.

Father Jack expressed concern about the absence of real community spirit in our parish and asked us – no, begged us – to dedicate time to pay regular visits to those who lived alone or were in need.

And then he did the unthinkable. He asked us to turn to the person next to us and hold their hand in the spirit of creating connection.

It was a Moses moment for sure.[10]

Most people looked horrified. Some parishioners scurried out, mumbling under their breath about what an idiot he was. Others simply ignored his request. Some of us remained, feeling a great deal of discomfort as we shuffled in our seats, wondering whether to be the one to make the first move.

What struck me, even back then, was how Father Jack's request of us, to hold the hand of our neighbour, was an act that was so foreign to us all. It was terrifying for some; character-defining for me.

As I turned to my right to extend my hand to my fellow parishioner, I noticed him for the first time. Small and hunched over, the elderly man was vision impaired. The lenses of his eyes were covered with a film of milky cloudiness, indicating the presence of inoperable cataracts. He grabbed onto my hand. His gnarled fingers clutched mine tight in a vice-like grip. I wondered how long it had been since he had felt the touch of another human being. My instincts told me: far too long.

**I realised that what nourishes the human spirit is not the pursuit of wealth or fame, but love.**

I realised that what nourishes the human spirit is not the pursuit of wealth or fame, but love. Through the forging of deep connection with each other and a commitment to a happy and meaningful life, we can create a world where love surrounds us all.

The truth is that Father Jack, the provocateur priest, was ahead of his time.

## THE REBIRTH OF RADICAL HUMANITY

The world is wounded.

The events of the past ten years have made it abundantly clear, if it wasn't already, that a volatile and complex world is resulting in casualties at an accelerating rate. We are caught in the crossfire of multiple existential crises.

From natural disasters and climate change to a world pandemic, digital disruption and catastrophic increases in mental ill health, humanity is buckling under the strain of modern-day advancement.

We are all standing at the edge of our most extreme challenge. We are being forced to rethink our approach to life and work, and find creative ways to amplify our ability to evolve. Being able to adapt to an unchartered future that involves both people and planet is mission critical if we are to remain on this earth.

It's time for a new leadership logic; one that is unreasonably ambitious, bold, adaptive and *radically human*. One that is capable of building thriving, prosperous and purposeful organisations during these transformational times. The world needs leaders who celebrate being radically human and worship the planet at the same time.

To get ready for what is to come, as a race we must move beyond resilience and simply coping. The greater challenge lies in building our ability to move fluidly between the two worlds of the present and the future, strengthened by challenge and adversity.

But first we must believe – because *believing is seeing*. We must trust in our ability to improvise, flex and morph to better withstand the shifting tides of turbulence and change.

But rising is uncomfortable. It is not an innate trait. It takes ferocious energy, an iron will and unwavering commitment to feeding the hunger that drives it.

How do you cultivate this?

How do you prepare yourself to be the best version of you?

The Japanese have a word for it: *ikigai* – 'reason for living'. The French call it *raison d'être* – 'reason for being'.

Everyone carries an *ikigai* within them. The evidence is undisputed: having a clearly defined purpose or greater calling brings elevated happiness, satisfaction and meaning to our lives. It's what sustains our energy and motivation, even during times when life seems bleak, and keeps our eyes on what matters most.

Discovering your *ikigai* is akin to turning on your inner pilot light to direct your energy and intention. This is where we must all begin.

## Reflection

- What gets you up out of bed in the morning?
- What 'calls' you the loudest?
- What's your *ikigai*?

## REINVENTING YOURSELF TO THRIVE

Stephen Quantrill, who we met in chapter 2, came from a crime-ridden and unsafe country. He left behind a successful life of privilege and status to come to a foreign culture and country with no safety net. He didn't know what awaited him. His wife had been endangered in South Africa, so an unwavering commitment to his purpose (to provide his family with a safe environment for them to flourish) was the driving force behind his actions.

No-one is inherently adaptive all the time. To be so is a fight against our own biology. Quantrill was able to nurture his unreasonable ambition and take a huge leap of faith to realise a new life for himself and his family. But it took everything in him to do so. He had to shed control, eliminate his own biases, demolish his need for status, trust his instincts and step into his full potential to *reinvent* himself.

I'm a big fan of Viktor Frankl. While there may be opposing views on the choices of this famous psychotherapist, he remains for me one of the most progressive thought leaders in human motivation. He said: 'Everything can be taken from a man but one thing: the last of the human freedoms – to choose one's attitude in any given circumstances, to choose one's own way.'

And that's what Quantrill did. He chose his mindset, he chose his path and he pursued it relentlessly until *it was*.

Leaders with unreasonable ambition live and die for their principles and ideals. They are prepared to make themselves a target and lead the way for others so that real change can happen.

They are the leaders with something to live for.

They are the heretics who die for the cause.

Martin Luther King's famous prophetic words come to my mind: 'If a man has not discovered something that he will die for, he is not fit to live.'

Amen.

## Reflection

·  What are the non-negotiable values and principles you live by?

·  What does the world need from you right now?

·  What cause would you 'die' for?

# CHAPTER 4

# THE UNREASONABLY AMBITIOUS LEADER

Our wretched species is so made that those who
walk on the well-trodden path always throw stones
at those who are showing a new road.

– VOLTAIRE

Love can make us do crazy things. It can fill us with the courage to take great risks and engage in extraordinary feats of bravery just to secure the heart of those we love (even if they may not feel the same way).

But what if following love saw you travelling halfway across the world, with little means and no place to live, then being dumped shortly after arriving? What would you do?

Well, let me introduce you to Nick. Because it happened to him. This is his story of how he followed, crashed, rose and triumphed. Nick is what I would call a walking, talking résumé of unreasonable ambition. To learn how he cultivated it, it helps to understand his origins. In working with my clients, that's always our departure gate for revealing the potential to *be more*.

Nick was raised in South Australia. At 24 he graduated with a business and marketing degree from Flinders University and went on to pursue a career in radio and media production. His father, Frank – a Greek-Italian immigrant, property developer and filmmaker – had been able to 'retire' early, and raised his son with his wife on their rural property in wine country, Port Willunga.

From his father Nick inherited the entrepreneurial gene, a strong immigrant work ethic and the ability to quickly see and exploit opportunities. His father was also creative, industrious and risqué, spending his days cold-pressing olive oil and making body casts of local pregnant women. He even had his pieces featured in a reputable art show (impressive, right?) and won prizes for his olive oil and gigantic kalamatas.

Down-to-earth and with a jovial and infectious energy, Nick had become skilled at building relationships with people from all walks of life. He'd watched his father making friends easily, calling people 'china' ('china plate' is a rhyming slang phrase for 'mate') and hosting regular wood-fired dinners for their wealthy neighbours. It was not uncommon to have famous artists, fashion designers even a newspaper magnate popping in to say hi over a glass of wine. This was great for Nick, an only child who appreciated the company and learned how to relate to just about anyone.

Nick's decision to follow his heart and move to London was a *big* move for the young man from Adelaide. It was a life-defining moment. He had already built up a name for himself as marketing director for some of South Australia's iconic entertainment properties. It was his work on *La Clique* cabaret show that secured him a gig with his friend, manager of the Hippodrome – a landmark in London's West End that is now home to an international-style casino – and cemented his decision to leave Australia and be with his girlfriend who had already moved there.

Four months after his landing, though, his relationship went south. With nowhere to live and prices for London rent skyrocketing, he accepted his friend's offer to move into an abandoned dressing room at the Hippodrome for a while.

This was a sliding-door moment for Nick. Working at the Hippodrome and living in the dressing room, he got to meet and build relationships with some of the most incredible starlets, performers and creatives. After a year of 'showering in the sink', he landed an intro-duction to Harvey Goldsmith – the music promoter who produced Live Aid, the biggest televised international charity event of our time, with Bob Geldof in 1985.

And the rest is history.

Nick became an events producer for some of the biggest names in the biz, such as Gucci and Beyonce's Chime for Change event. He married a gorgeous Parisian Crazy Horse showgirl and now runs a successful entertainment production company. Nick combines his love of food and music to produce unique experiences for his guests at iconic locations around the world. He even had an artist paint his dad wearing a sombrero on a mural in one of his restaurants!

In getting to know Nick over many decades (I've known him since we were children), what I have observed is that he has been cultivating his gifts and talents over a lifetime. He will tell you that he is not that clever, and that he is just lucky (he is extremely self-effacing). He'll say he not the most gifted 'ranga'[11] on the planet; he just knows what people want, and how to get them 'fired up'.

Certainly luck has had some part to play in Nick's story but the real secret behind his success is his *mindset*.

## MINDSET MATTERS MOST

Mindset is everything. Your mindset can amplify or destroy your chances at living your best life.

That may sound a tad dramatic, but I promise you I am being very straight with you. Mindset is the primary reason why most large-scale organisational transformation efforts fail.

Think about it. Why do organisations fail at transformation? They've got a clear direction, clever people, resources and good systems. It should be foolproof, right?

They fail because they focus on the *doing* of transformation without the culture or mindset to support the change – the *being*. The doing is the easy part. It's about implementing policies, procedures and processes to support new ways of working and delivering value to customers. It's relying on current logic and what we know to create improvements. It's focusing on the known knowns and unknown knowns.

But there are also *unknown unknowns* – things we don't know we don't know – and that's where *being* becomes paramount.

And here's the rub: without there being a shift in thinking and being, and without leaders doing the psychological heavy lifting to build environments where people are agile, empowered and able to harness their full creative potential, efforts prove futile.

This was put to the test in 2015 by a guy very well known in the agility space: Steve Denning. Denning put together a team of equally impressive academics and journeyed around the world, visiting loads of different organisations. His research question was simple: in a tech-driven economy, do leaders need a fundamental makeover? He wanted to investigate the fundamental differences between organisations that had successfully transformed and those that had not.

What he uncovered was startling. He found that the universal feature of transformation success was the leadership mindset. Where new processes, technologies and systems were implemented without the right mindset, no benefits were observed.[12]

*What you think matters.* No matter the context, personal or work life, the same priority applies.

How committed are you to setting up your mindset for success? Here are some questions to help you answer this question.

## Reflection

- How do you evaluate your own frame of mind?

- How do you train your brain to maximise your potential and maintain your effectiveness no matter the 'weather' conditions?

- Are you able to recognise the old records playing in your head, or the limiting beliefs preventing you from enjoying the success and fulfilment you deserve?

- Where are you relying on outdated ways of leading and engaging that stifle your team's contributions and greater efforts?

- How are you leading to make your people awesome?

## WHAT DOES AN UNREASONABLY AMBITIOUS MINDSET LOOK LIKE?

Answering these questions is important. If you understand your baseline you will be able to figure out the *size* of your mindset challenge, and how hard you'll have to work to fill the gaps.

Let's face it: Nick could be deemed the poster man for an unreasonably ambitious leader. His approach to life and circumstances illustrates just how much having an agile mindset and taking adaptive action equates to success.

Today, the new world order has changed the rules on us yet again. But the challenge remains the same. Defining your version of success and choosing which of your gifts to leverage to get there is the only way – if you want to flourish.

So just how did Nick, a regular guy from Adelaide, know how to harness his mental agility and become future-ready?

Nick's brain had been trained over decades to adapt during periods of radical change and great unknowns. This primed him to deftly wrestle with the uncertain future that lay before him.

I've reflected on this a lot over the last 20 years, observing leaders like Nick. I'd like to use him as an example to outline the attributes I have seen consistently show up in leaders with unreasonable ambition. It's these ten attributes that I believe set unreasonably ambitious leaders apart:

1. **Driven and speedy:** Nick has a relentless focus on the end game. He seizes opportunities and moves fast. He is emboldened through execution – making action happen. He doesn't wait for moss to grow.

2. **Agile and restless:** He's independent, daring and hungry for progress.

3. **Gritty and tenacious:** Nick is energised by monumental challenges and death-defying setbacks. He stays the course no matter what. Fear and doubt motivate higher performance and spark creative adaptation.

4. **Delusional:** Nick has a rockstar mentality. He's a realist but he also knows he is awesome and gives everything a go. He trusts his ability to figure things out even if he doesn't have all the answers.

5. **A rebel with a cause:** He flourishes in discomfort and ambiguity. He plays by his own rules to have impact that counts, and makes a real difference.

6. **Unconstrained:** He is a creative visionary who imagines the future without limits. He's a little 'out there'; some may even call him 'weird' or 'unorthodox'.

7. **Passionate and inspiring:** Nick is ridiculously passionate and inspires others to action. He's a high-energy guy who knows how to motivate and influence.

8. **Humble and genuine:** He takes a direct approach and speaks up whether you like it or not. Being able to maintain a sense of humour and crack jokes is one of his greatest attributes.

9. **An adventure-seeker:** Nick is voraciously curious and attracted to the thrill of his next adventure. He's motivated by being an early mover and will take big jumps to get there.

10. **A sense of wonder and possibility:** Nick believes in 'magic' and miracles. He lives a life of awe, wonder and limitless possibility. He relies heavily on intuition.

With the world in a state of exponential flux and life as we know it morphing at warp speed, it will take the unreasonably ambitious misfits like Nick – the square pegs in round holes, the believers, the visionaries and the dreamers – to shake up the modern world and pave the way for future generations. As Steve Jobs said, 'The people who are crazy enough to think they can change the world are the ones who do.'

Simply put, I believe there are two roads to success:

1. Become beige-coloured wallpaper, blending into a dominant world view, with your talents delivering mild impact and mediocrity.

2. Speak up and stand out to move the world in a new direction. This means being ready to show up to the party and back yourself to lead.

Option 2 is not for the meek. But ask just about any unreasonably ambitious leader which option they would pick, and you will discover it is *not* a choice for them; it is a way of being. They would be unreasonably ambitious, irrespective of the consequences. Because that's just *who they are*.

To create a life of *unreasonable ambition* means:

· being prepared to fight for who you are and claim your place at the table without apology
· withstanding the harshest critics to stay true to yourself
· accepting the downside of being unreasonably ambitious – because it's who you are.

So, what is that downside? Think of the expression 'the higher you rise, the further you fall'. We'll talk more about that in chapter 5, when we meet Raphaël Lapointe and hear his story.

## Reflection

- Are you ready to show up and claim your space without apology?

- What are you prepared to fight for?

- How would you rate yourself on the ten unreasonably ambitious leader attributes? (Give yourself a score, with ten being 'yes, I have nailed it!', five being 'I am halfway there' and one being 'yeah, not at all'.)

# CHAPTER 5

# THE DARK SIDE OF UNREASONABLE AMBITION

I like the night. Without the dark,
we'd never see the stars.

– STEPHENIE MEYER

We've all heard of *Twilight* – the teen vampire love story that depicts the inevitable collision of star-crossed lovers. A reformed blood-sucking vampire ('evil') falls for his alter ego: the girl-next-door, virgin mortal who dances to the beat of her own drum ('good'). The Twilight Saga films, based on Stephenie Meyer's bestselling books, were so successful they smashed box-office sales and have been touted as Hollywood's most successful film franchise.

I believe the reason so many were invested in this story is because, at an unconscious level, we are psychologically attracted to understanding the two parts of our human mind: the light and the shadow. The light self represents the best and most positive parts of ourselves (the conscious). The shadow self represents wildness, chaos and the unknown (the unconscious).

People who are unreasonably ambitious are often exceptional; but their gifts can sometimes come at a price. It's the quintessential leveller; kind of like the universe seeking to balance out the dark and the light.

The unreasonably ambitious could be described as representing a higher form of human evolution and self-actualisation. Self-actualisation is an ideal that humanity is striving to realise, consciously or not. It represents the highest level of psychological development, the light self, where personal potential is fully realised.

My former esteemed professor, Rogerian psychotherapist Dr Godfrey Barrett-Lennard, described self-actualisation as 'striving to become as close to Christ-like as possible'. I always found this to be a lofty aspiration for flawed and imperfect creatures such as us, and yet some might conclude that the unreasonably ambitious are driven to transcend the limits of their 'mortal' existence.

But just like in the olden days, when nonconformists and original thinkers were labelled and cast out as witches, the *unreasonably ambitious* can also command negative attention and are often 'burnt at the stake' in one way or another. Dancing to the beat of your own drum doesn't mean everyone is dancing with you.

**Dancing to the beat of your own drum doesn't mean everyone is dancing with you.**

After working with *unreasonably ambitious* leaders for so long I've seen how their commitment to living life as their authentic selves can come at great personal cost. And yet they don't know how to do life any other way. As one Silicon Valley tech leader once said to me, 'It's worth the temporary moments of pain, because to live my life any other way would be to sell my soul to the highest bidder and not be aligned with my purpose.'

## FALLING FROM GRACE

*How the mighty have fallen and the weapons of war*
*have perished! Oh, how the mighty heroes have fallen!*
*Stripped of their weapons, they lie dead.*

– Samuel 1:27

While working in Ottawa for five years I witnessed an unreasonably ambitious leader's fallout firsthand. It wasn't just a mild trip-up; it was an almighty tumbling from the top of the Laurentian Mountains.

Raphaël Lapointe is a charismatic, outspoken and visionary leader. His hire as the youngest director general in the region (he was 37) was an unconventional move for the hyperconservative president of the Desjardins Credit Union.[13] To put it mildly, his appointment into one of the top banking jobs in Outaouais region was not well received by the broader French Canadian banking community.

You see, Lapointe was all about change. The French Canadian banking industry was a powerful and prehistoric beast. As the largest employer in Québec, Desjardins led its business and its people with a top-down approach while maintaining a low-key but well-known allegiance to driving its nationalist political agenda. And Lapointe was a renegade leader who did not play by the rules (you can understand why they may have been nervous!).

Lapointe had worked his way up the food chain, turning around smaller credit unions in rural areas until he got noticed. He was the kind of guy who rolled his sleeves up and got in the trenches with his people. He rebuilt retail banking outposts from the ground up to make them financially viable, turning them into communities that employees were proud to be part of. After working with him for more than two years, I could tell that his earlier successes could be attributed to a few key strengths: his powers of persuasion, his ability to inspire the troops and his stubborn bias for action. He was smooth, but not smarmy; clever, but still cool. He was a relatable connector who could charm the pants off even the most hostile contender.

I liken the story of Lapointe's rapid demise to the story of Icarus, from Greek mythology. Perhaps you've heard of it?

Icarus was the son of Daedalus. He tried to escape Crete by wearing a pair of wings his father created. Daedalus warned him not to fly too close to the sun, lest his wings melt; but he disregarded the warning and plunged to his death, drowning in the sea below. The story is a reminder that hubris (excessive pride and self-confidence) can blind us from making good decisions, and even lead to our demise.

Like Icarus, Lapointe had everything to gain from taking big risks – which he did naturally, without too much thought about the perils of doing so. He was born into an underprivileged *quartier* in Montréal; his father drove taxis, and his mother earnt a few extra dollars by waiting tables at a suburban diner. Lapointe had been sent out to work early – at ten years old he started delivering papers around his neighbourhood on a pushbike to help his family out.

Given this, it may surprise you that what impressed me the most about Lapointe was not his title and power, nor his magnetism, but his poise and class. Having come from a middle-class family myself I assumed that he had, too. His manners were impeccable; his voice eloquent and articulate. To this day, I can honestly say I have never met anyone who has appeared as gifted by circumstance as him. It was as if Professor Henry Higgins had taken him in and prepared him for a life of high society.[14]

And *that* was the problem.

Lapointe was playing the charade of the person he thought he *ought to be*. He wasn't being authentic, and this limited the trust others gave him. It led to a perception of him having questionable integrity.

In his quest for growth and realising his full potential he became a victim of his own success. He failed to notice the cues around him signalling that a *coup d'état* was being staged and that he would eventually be ousted from the bank under a shroud of questionable ethics.

I saw the signs and warned him of trouble brewing. I could sense what was to come and encouraged him to get out before the hurricane hit. I tried to prepare him for an inevitable exit on his terms. He listened to me, at first – going back to university and enrolling in his MBA to become more market-ready (he already had a degree in political science). He could see what was happening but didn't act on it – believing it would all eventually blow over (he is a super optimist).

It was his delusions of grandeur and inflated idealism that left him ill-prepared to deal with a reputation in tatters after an ousting of gigantic proportions.

It was horrific to watch.

One day in the summer of 2006 this unreasonably ambitious leader went from having his face plastered on billboards at the hockey stadium to being chased out of Ottawa. He was blacklisted and no-one would employ him, despite his great success and impressive skillset.

But let's pause for a moment. Both Nick and Lapointe are unreasonably ambitious leaders. They share many of the same attributes and their stories of origin are similar. So, what went wrong for Lapointe? Why did Nick's career skyrocket, while Lapointe's plunged into a toilet bowl?

Lapointe's story is a harsh example of what can happened to an unreasonably ambitious leader who goes off track. His story illustrates how being unreasonably ambitious can also make you a target for judgement and scepticism; how it can derail you if you don't pay attention and learn how to navigate the ecosystem that surrounds you.

Lapointe's experience teaches us that if an unreasonably ambitious leader is to succeed, bloom and prosper they must also carefully manage any associated risks and consciously handle the environment they are operating in.

Specifically, there are five lessons all unreasonably ambitious leaders must take to heart if they're to avoid a similar fall from grace.

### Lesson 1: Political agility

Being a bold explorer prepared to challenge the status quo puts the unreasonably ambitious leader into the spotlight, whether they like it or not. Learning how to rally the troops to gather support and navigate the political landscape is critical to your success. Being able to effectively garner the support of allies at every level is paramount to being able to influence change.

### Lesson 2: Envisioning and engagement

Voracious curiosity, drive and speed were all part of Lapointe's makeup. Learning to slow down and spend time selling the vision and promoting a direction would have optimised team engagement and created transparency in the execution of outcomes. If people feel excluded or they don't know you, they will fill in the blanks with assumptions that are usually not true.

### Lesson 3: Transparency and collaboration

Driving results alone instead of collaborating with others led to Lapointe's efforts being misinterpreted, resulting in him being cast out. Lapointe spent most of his time barking orders from his mobile phone and little time in the office. He was frequently out at long lunches, meeting with VIPs and drinking expensive bottles of wine. Few had oversight over his dealings, and nobody could vouch for his productivity or articulate his value or contributions.

### Lesson 4: Engaging hearts and minds

Lapointe's creative, exuberant energy and innovative ideas made him ahead of his time – and this scared people. His reaction to their fear was to become frustrated and bullish, which finally split the ranks against him. Becoming forceful and commanding when under pressure won't win the war; and without investment into relationships, the loyalty for his leadership was precarious at best.

## Lesson 5: Humility and vulnerability

Lapointe's overconfidence led to his final undoing. Staying humble and more actively asking for feedback may have helped him keep his finger on the pulse of how others really viewed him. Allowing himself to be vulnerable and show his humanity would have allowed others to connect with him more deeply.

### Show up as you are

The truth was, no-one really knew who Lapointe was. What they experienced instead was a version of him – a social mask he donned to meet expectations.

Like many unreasonably ambitious leaders I have worked with over the years, Lapointe was, at his core, a closet introvert playing at being sociable. He shared with me once that his dream life was to live a solitary existence in a cottage in the middle of a forest far away from people. His favourite winter hobby was to ice skate by himself, pushing a hockey puck around a frozen pond. He told me it's when he did his best thinking.

To be honest, when I heard this, I could hardly imagine it. His social front as a bullish extrovert was so well crafted and his true self so well hidden it was a challenge even for me to imagine it. And then, one night after a networking event at a hotel in Lac Carling, I happened to look out of the window and saw him outside. He was a dancer on ice, effortlessly gliding around a pond amid a fluttering of falling snow.

I was speechless. It was in this moment that I knew I had finally seen the 'real' Lapointe.

And he was beautiful.

There is no doubt that to be unreasonably ambitious can sometimes be a tough journey, but it *does not have to be*. I've often wondered how, if Lapointe had shown himself to his people, that might have changed his fate.

Conventional leadership development wisdom says that we should leverage and capitalise on our strengths. Lapointe's story is a reminder of what happens when an exceptionally talented leader with unreasonable ambition overuses their strengths, becoming a liability.

Compounded by his unwillingness to show his true character, it sent him off-kilter and diminished his capacity to gain support and lead.

Having unreasonable ambition is important, but it is not the only ingredient to build a meaningful life. Behaviours, decisions and actions must also be anchored in strong values and a lifetime commitment to personal growth and evolution.

At a fundamental level, Lapointe was missing three key things: acute self-awareness, self-acceptance and a deeper connection to a greater life purpose.

Just as with any skyscraper that is built to last, human beings must also start with solid foundations.

In part II: mantra, we will explore how to build a set of life-affirming principles to strengthen a rock-solid core from which to navigate your own unique path and stay the course, no matter how shaky the rattling may become.

## Reflection

- Do you view politics as a necessary evil or avoid it altogether? Being able to navigate the twists and turns of organisational life as a leader means walking the tightrope and balancing critical relationships to influence outcomes.

- Do you sacrifice relationships for results, seeing 'small talk' as a waste of time?

- How do you maintain your openness and accessibility?

- Think about times when you get defensive. It's probably your ego squawking as your self-worth comes under fire. Think about why the situation is causing fear in you. Ask yourself, is my reaction to this disproportionate to the threat? What's really going on here?

- How would others describe you? Are you a different person at home and at work? If you are, why do you feel a need to change yourself? How far is too far away from the real you?

# PART II

# MAN

# TRA

Somewhere, something incredible is waiting
to be known.

– BLAISE PASCAL

Julie was the well-known CEO of a technology company in Ottawa. Ottawa is the picturesque capital city of Canada, known for having the world's longest ice-skating rink – Rideau Canal (7.8 km) – and the most spectacular tulip displays in the country. If you haven't been, it's like being on a Disney set with its majestic château-like buildings, reminiscent of a bygone era. It's a very romantic town.

When I met Julie, her life was far from being a fairy tale. She was amid personal upheaval, going through a bitter divorce. Her spouse, who was in a lower-level leadership role at his work, was going after her for financial recompense to make up for the 'decrease in quality of life' that would eventuate because of their dissolution of marriage.

It was difficult to coach Julie. Not because she wasn't a talented and engaging CEO, but because her mind wasn't able to be fully present to receive the insights from our work; nor did she have the energy to apply them. Her brain was too full trying to navigate her personal life. The guilt she felt around making the decision to leave her husband of 20 years played heavily on her mind. She tied herself up in knots, wrestling with her next move, feeling like a horrible person for 'hurting' him and leaving him 'alone'.

I empathised with where she was at, having struggled with years of self-torment when my own 'forever' marriage to my university sweet-heart blew up after a few short years (Catholic guilt guarantees you years of torment!). One of the most powerful mental tools I developed to get through was my practice of mantras – also known as positive affirmations. Now, I can appreciate that this is all sounding a little 'woo-woo', particularly for a hardcore high-performance coach like me. But believe me: it isn't as crazy as it sounds. As a positive psychologist I know that the healing power of reciting daily mantras is a tried-and-tested mind power tool to help humans quickly raise their level of consciousness to an elevated state of happiness.

The use of mantras to boost our mental state to optimism is not a new-age fad. It has quite the illustrious spiritual history and has been around for centuries. In India a mantra is considered sacred and passed on from a 'guru' to their 'disciple'. Today, in Western society, research has demonstrated that mantras said out loud can shift emotions towards a positive mindset and energy towards intentional action. The vast amount of data that backs this up speaks to its therapeutic impact.[15]

A good way to imagine the effect of having a mantra to guide your daily mindset and rituals is to think about how you feel when you read a favourite quote that you love. Why do you love it? How does it make you feel? Why does it resonate so strongly?

If you're like me, you probably find yourself saving favourite quotes to read again later. It's because the words you are reading are connecting with something deep within you – perhaps it is an experience you are going through in the present moment, one that you have lived through in the past, or maybe it represents a future state – something you aspire to or dream about. Whatever it triggers in you, it is powerful because it speaks to the essence of who you are and what you desire the most.

In that moment, it's as if you are *seen, heard and understood.*

Whether it be that favourite quote that has caught your attention, song lyrics or a poem that you love, psychologists know that when you speak, your words carry great power. Even left-brained, tech-CEO Julie managed to unearth a life-guiding mantra that anchored her to the present and helped her override the limiting beliefs that were echoing in her head about her own self-worth for ending her toxic relationship. Her mantra was: 'I know that I am exactly where I need to be and that I am enough. When the time is right, I know that love will find me.'

Building mantra rituals enabled Julie to get through the darkness of her divorce and focus her energy on creating a new life for herself that was more aligned with her future.

In this part of the book we are going to deconstruct how to build the psychological bricks and mortar for continued success, before you take your mind to the gym to do the heavy lifting in part III: mindset. To build our strongest unwavering foundation we need three fundamental ingredients to drive our efforts as unreasonably ambitious leaders: self-awareness, self-love and clarity of purpose.

To build our foundation we need three ingredients: self-awareness, self-love and clarity of purpose.

Anchoring your mindset with unreasonably ambitious roots always begins with the most basic of human questions: who are you?

Knowing yourself is where your core, your internal engine, generates a sustainable source of power for you to flourish – no matter what is happening around you. Knowing what you stand for and the intention that drives your actions harnesses the energy to make action happen. Being committed to honouring the life you aspire to create for yourself is what keeps you on track, no matter how unwieldy life's twists and turns.

I invite you to take my hand and begin by exploring some of the fundamentals to building an unshakeable inner core.

# CHAPTER 6

# KNOW THYSELF

There are three extremely hard things in this world:
steel, diamonds, and to know oneself.

– BENJAMIN FRANKLIN

*Who are you?*

Don't you just *hate* that question? I know I do.

I hate it because it is a hard question. I hate it because it is a scary question. I hate it because it forces me to go to the deepest parts of myself to answer it. I hate it because to reveal the answer means I must reveal my true self – my private self that I keep buried and hidden from the world more than I share it.

It's why writing this book has been such a painstaking process. Because to be true to myself, to be true to you, dear reader, I must show up, fully.

And that is terrifying to me.

But I know that I am not alone in my fear. I believe that doing the work to know ourselves and choosing to lead with *who we are*, not with *what we know* or *what we do,* is the springboard for unlocking our full potential and waking up that sleeping giant that is waiting to be set free.

## BATTLING WHO YOU ARE

I'll never forget meeting Dominic (Dom) Sheldrick. He was tall and striking, and his blue eyes twinkled as he greeted me with a firm yet kind handshake in the lobby of the organisational development firm I had joined upon my return from North America. What struck me about Sheldrick was his intensity; he emanated an almost otherworldly aura.

Sheldrick was introduced to me as an executive coach the company I worked for was wooing to support the demand of a growing organisational development practice. I was intrigued from the first 'hello'. He wasn't like anyone else I had met since my return to Perth. There was something different about his energy that made him stand out from the rest – I just couldn't put my finger on it.

And then I discovered his magic. I came to understand his uniqueness, the edge that he brought to his work. And it all made sense.

I found out that Sheldrick had been an elite swimmer. He had dedicated more than half his life preparing for one goal: to win the Olympic gold. But life didn't end up the way he had planned. Sheldrick was diagnosed with leukaemia shortly after he missed making the selection into the 1988 Seoul Olympic Games. What is impressive about his story is the grit he showed to heal and return to competitive swimming and try to make the 1992 Barcelona Olympic Games. It didn't happen for Sheldrick, but his leukaemia never came back.

Now, as a motivational speaker, Sheldrick has spent years telling the powerful and inspiring story of how he overcome his battle with cancer to return to a passion he loved. But for me, there is another story that is even more compelling than his experience dealing with a life-threatening illness – one to which more of us might be able to relate.

And it's this: the story of how Sheldrick lost himself after making his way back from the brink. How swimming was the only working life that he had known, and having to leave it resulted in a complete fracturing of who he thought he was – and what he had to offer the world.

It's a story of how an elite sportsman ended up working for one of the local shires watering plants from a truck on a newly created freeway, not knowing where to go or what to do next. At the time, Sheldrick couldn't see himself through any other lens than athleticism. His entire self-worth was tied up in those Speedos he had worn for so long – but they didn't fit him any more. Sheldrick had to rediscover all the other parts of himself that made him who he was – a whole person, not just Sheldrick the swimmer.

It's a recurring issue I see for so many I work with. Their self-worth and identity is tied almost singularly to the work that they do, not the complete person they are. And it ties them up in knots. It can create disconnect, and even destroy other aspects of their lives, if they focus all their energy on building their work persona.

## YOU ARE SO MUCH MORE

Getting to the core of recognising the many parts of who you are is not something many of us think about – because being able to understand your own essence takes *insight* and *sweat*.

I am a big fan of social psychologist Mark Snyder's work investigating why so many leaders believe they must present as two different people in life – at home and at work. Sheldrick's story is powerful in teaching us about the slippery slope of what Snyder calls *self-monitoring* – choosing to present only a fragment of who we are – and how this can erode our ability to flourish by distorting accurate perceptions of self.[16] Self-monitoring is a personality trait that involves the ability to monitor and regulate self-presentation, emotions and behaviours in response to social environments and situations. People high in self-monitoring are likely to change their behaviours to adapt or conform to a situation. They are chameleons.

So, I am going to ask you that dreaded question again:

*Who are you?*

When you answer, reflect on the many parts of yourself through the lens of the multiple identities that you have (which is completely normal, by the way!). Then I want you to go deeper and think about the beautiful, complex petals of the flower you are unfurling (that's you by the way) by asking yourself the following questions.

## Reflection

· What gifts do you bring to this world?

· What unique talents and skills do you possess?

· What do you value?

· What are you *not*?

· Are you showing up fully, both privately and publicly?

· Are you living a life that showcases the best parts of yourself?

Sheldrick was a well-known athlete, yes, but he was also a brother, a son, a friend, a husband, and later a father of four. Sheldrick's real work was to build a more accurate portrait of who he was – at his best and at his worst – and embrace all parts of himself.

If you are wondering where to start on your unreasonably ambitious leadership journey, I hope the first step has become clear.

Self-awareness is your greatest superpower. To become an unreasonably ambitious leader is to *know who you are*. To do this requires you to conduct a sobering audit of the internal resources you've got to work with; and then surround yourself with an entourage that fills in the gaps.

What is so profound about Sheldrick's story is that it teaches us that sometimes you have to lose yourself to find your way. I am certain just about everyone can relate to this. We have all at some point in our lives experienced moments of madness, to our benefit and to our detriment. What matters is how we unravel that big ball of string called life to get back to the essence of who we are.

---

**Sometimes you have to lose yourself to find your way.**

---

We have to remember that when all is said and done, it doesn't matter what *others* say about us, or how *they* define success. What matters is your own judgement of yourself, because 'knowing yourself is true wisdom' (thanks Lao Tzu) and, in my view, the only yardstick by which to live.

Knowing who you are also means knowing how you lead. And that's where we're headed next.

# CHAPTER 7

# BRING ME A HIGHER LOVE

One day Alice came to a fork in the road and
saw a Cheshire cat in a tree. 'Which road do I take?'
she asked. 'Where do you want to go?' was his response.
'I don't know,' Alice answered. 'Then,' said the cat,
'it doesn't matter. Any road will get you there.'

– LEWIS CARROLL

Lezly was so gruff on the phone I almost hung up. She had signed up to participate in one of my leadership transformation programs and was already proving to be a nightmare. My business partner was worried that her presence might potentially disrupt the dynamic of the program and ruin the experience for the other participants. I asked my partner to trust my judgement. I understood why my partner was nervous but we hadn't evaluated Lezly's leadership potential yet; we didn't have enough objective data to make a call on her suitability to the program so we decided to hold off on a final call.

What I uncovered next blew me away.

Lezly was a young, bright superstar bulldozing her way through relationships and recruitment business to achieve roaring financial success ($60 million revenue in 18 months), burning people and herself in the process. Her relentless drive originated in a history of having nothing; a past of sexual abuse and trauma, living with her grandparents, estranged from her drug-addicted mother. She had something to prove to the world: that she was something, and *nothing* would get in her way.

Lezly presented as a bad-arse entrepreneur: combative, argumentative and void of any real compassion. She was always in fight mode, fists at the ready, words armed to strike. Other people's reactions to her were starkly visible, particularly in meetings. Chairs rolled back away from the table, backs stiffened and silence descended as her presence darkened the mood of group gatherings. Everyone was just a little on edge, waiting for her to strike.

In Lezly's mind, others were simply responding to her magnetic energy – shaking in their own inferiority in the company of such a warrior woman and too intimidated to speak. She couldn't have been more wrong. Lezly was the biggest blocker to her own evolution. Celebrating her own 'cult of self'[17], she became increasingly self-absorbed and less self-aware.

As I peeled away her layers, I discovered the source of the misdirection: Lezly was struggling to be seen. Too afraid to surrender her ego, she had built a ten-foot wall around herself to hide her real self – fierce and vulnerable, strong and quivering, driven and afraid.

I can recall the exact moment the shift happened in her; that instant when the light went on, the glimmer that sparkled across her face.

We were having an insights session. This is when I take an 'x-ray' of my clients' minds to figure out what makes them tick, using a psychometric test. It's powerful stuff. I learn about what motivates other humans, what their strengths are and how they are using them (or not); what holds them back from stepping into their full potential.

The moment I spoke the truth to her about what I was seeing, the shift in Lezly happened almost instantaneously. I asked her why someone so loving and kind was pushing herself so far away from what she wanted most in her life – to love and be loved. I pointed out that her hard edge and aggressive persona were creating an unintended consequence: people were backing away from her, as if holding a crucifix to ward off an imminent vampire attack.

And that's when it sank in.

She didn't behave like someone whose core values were love, empathy, connection and belonging. In truth, those things were what she craved the most. They were the cornerstones of the business she wanted to build, and how she wanted to lead. And yet she wasn't living or feeling those values.

Working on understanding your values is such important work, and the next step in setting up a solid launchpad from which to catapult your authentic self. Becoming clear on your values and living them is *non-negotiable* if you want to be your best, most authentic self. The key is also to keep exploring them.

---

**Living your values is *non-negotiable* if you want to be your best, most authentic self.**

---

The absolute beauty of being human is that we evolve and change over time – as do our values, in reflection of our ongoing growth. To stay centred and true to our values, it's important to check in on our continued alignment with them. When we don't do this, we experience a situation like Lezly's – an enormous disconnect between her real intentions and how she was showing up. Psychologists have a term for this: *cognitive dissonance*. In simple terms, it's when your actions and words don't match up; when you are seen as a walking contradiction. It's one of the fastest ways for a leader to lose their people's trust. People notice when things are 'off'.

For Lezly, having empathy and love as two of her guiding north stars meant rethinking her approach to running her business and how she was leading herself and others. We worked on how she could rework her business strategy by putting people first. Her leadership style shifted from arrogant to humble, from domineering to inclusive, from profit-driven to heart-focused.

Lezly has also gone through a personal metamorphosis – she is barely recognisable as the woman I met nine months prior to the program. She has dropped almost 30 kilograms, left a marriage she was miserable in, and is focused on doing the healing to rejuvenate her soul and find her way back to her best self. Lezly has embraced all of who she is, moving to a place of acceptance and celebration for the person she is.

## Reflection

- How do you proactively seek out feedback on your own style and impact?

- If you don't do this, what is stopping you? What do you fear most about asking?

- Would people that know you describe you as having alignment between your private self and your public face? How well do people really know you?

- What work do you need to do on your own acceptance of self? Have you done the work to identify what you like most about yourself – your passions, your true motivations? How would others know this about you?

- What do you need to be doing more of to showcase all of you and what you stand for?

## KNOWING WHAT YOU STAND FOR

There are specific techniques that I use to help guide people back to their essence. With Lezly it was about reigniting her inner pilot light that had been temporality snuffed out by some traumatic life experiences.

It starts with going back to basics: identifying the life-guiding values that fuel the engine of your humanity. These values drive your thoughts, behaviours and actions.

Are you ready to give it a try?

(I encourage you to do this exercise if you haven't ever done it or if it's been a while. Values can shift as we do over time, so it's important to check in on where we are at regularly).

The secret to this exercise is to do it twice.

I've included a list of values on the following page. Look at the list and think about work. *What are your core guiding values at work?* Once you have selected these from the list, write down what behaviours you display that demonstrate your values at work.

Now, think about your personal life. *What are your core guiding values in your personal life?* Again, list the behaviours you display to showcase your personal values.

Now compare the two sets of values. Are they the same, or different? Chances are they are different. If they are, you're like many of the awesome leaders I work with. Know that you are not alone.

There's a recurring, entrenched belief that we need to be two different people at home and at work. It comes from a history of deep-rooted social programming (parental influences, culture and religion and our own biases); records that play in our head telling us to wear different social masks for different occasions.

If we are brave enough to take a dip into our emotional well, we learn that *shaky self-worth* is at the root of our anxiety and fear around fully showing ourselves. It's feeling like who we are is not enough; that to be accepted and fit in requires us to hide parts of who we really are. In doing so, we diminish our own power and create a life where we don't ever really belong.

## Core guiding values

| | | | | |
|---|---|---|---|---|
| Acceptance | Cooperation | Generosity | Motivation | Sincerity |
| Accomplishment | Courage | Geniusness | Openness | Skillfulness |
| Accountability | Courtesy | Giving | Optimism | Smartness |
| Accuracy | Creation | Goodness | Order | Solitude |
| Achievement | Creativity | Grace | Organisation | Spirit |
| Adaptability | Credibility | Gratitude | Originality | Spirituality |
| Alertness | Curiosity | Greatness | Passion | Spontaneousness |
| Altruism | Decisiveness | Growth | Patience | Stability |
| Ambition | Dedication | Happiness | Peace | Status |
| Amusement | Dependability | Hard work | Performance | Stewardship |
| Assertiveness | Determination | Harmony | Persistence | Strength |
| Attentiveness | Development | Health | Playfulness | Structure |
| Awareness | Devotion | Honesty | Poise | Success |
| Balance | Dignity | Honour | Potential | Support |
| Beauty | Discipline | Hope | Power | Surprise |
| Boldness | Discovery | Humility | Presence | Sustainability |
| Bravery | Drive | Imagination | Productivity | Talent |
| Brilliance | Effectiveness | Improvement | Professionalism | Teamwork |
| Calmness | Efficiency | Independence | Prosperity | Temperance |
| Candor | Empathy | Individuality | Purpose | Thankfulness |
| Capability | Empowerment | Innovation | Quality | Thoroughness |
| Carefulness | Endurance | Inquisitiveness | Realism | Thoughtfulness |
| Certainty | Energy | Insightfulness | Reason | Timeliness |
| Challenge | Enjoyment | Inspiration | Recognition | Tolerance |
| Charity | Enthusiasm | Integrity | Recreation | Toughness |
| Cleanliness | Equality | Intelligence | Reflection | Tradition |
| Clarity | Ethics | Intensity | Respect | Tranquility |
| Cleverness | Excellence | Intuition | Responsibility | Transparency |
| Comfort | Experience | Irreverence | Restraint | Trust |
| Commitment | Exploration | Joy | Results | Trustworthiness |
| Common sense | Expression | Justice | Reverence | Truth |
| Communication | Fairness | Kindness | Rigour | Understanding |
| Community | Fame | Knowledge | Risk | Uniqueness |
| Compassion | Family | Lawfulness | Satisfaction | Unity |
| Competence | Fearlessness | Leadership | Security | Valour |
| Concentration | Feelings | Learning | Self-reliance | Victory |
| Confidence | Ferociousness | Liberty | Selflessness | Vigour |
| Connection | Fidelity | Logic | Sensitivity | Vision |
| Consciousness | Focus | Love | Serenity | Vitality |
| Consistency | Foresight | Loyalty | Service | Wealth |
| Contentment | Fortitude | Mastery | Sharing | Welcoming |
| Contribution | Freedom | Maturity | Significance | Winning |
| Control | Friendship | Meaning | Silence | Wisdom |
| Conviction | Fun | Moderation | Simplicity | Wonder |

Now, back to the exercise. If your values between work and your personal life differ, try integrating the two sets so you have one set of values that represents your core self, no matter the context.

These are the values I encourage you to lead with.

Unreasonably ambitious leaders are not immutable. They are human, after all. But a key source of their power comes from holding one set of values for life, irrespective of context – that's what grounds them. They hold true to *who they are,* whether others like them or not; no matter how hard it gets or how much it may cost them.

It's their super strength.

## OPENING YOUR KIMONO

Now more than ever, people don't want to follow airbrushed leaders. In a world that is hyperfocused on fakeness (fake news, perfect lives, plastic bodies, plastered smiles), being real is rare. Authenticity has become prized, and authentic leaders highly sought after.

> Being real is rare. Authenticity has become prized.

It's the willingness to step out from behind the curtains and unmask their true selves that gives unreasonably ambitious leaders the ability to more powerfully engage others, in both life and at the office.

To do this takes extraordinary courage: the courage to face up to uncertainty as your genuine self; the courage to welcome the disruption going on around us, and see it as an opportunity to be better; the courage to put *believing before seeing.*

Lezly is a great example of a person who has stripped off the armour holding her back and seized the moment to reinvent herself. She's even launched a new side hustle, offering in-your-face coaching to help other leaders become more grounded as businesspeople while unashamedly embracing and sharing their most private selves with the world.

Now that you know who you are and what you stand for, let's explore how to push yourself and redefine your boundaries of what's possible for sustained success; to channel energy into creating momentum to forge your own path.

# CHAPTER 8

# COMMIT TO YOUR FUTURE SELF

When we can no longer change a situation,
we are challenged to change ourselves.

– VIKTOR FRANKL

If there is one thing I have learned as an organisational psychologist over the past couple of decades it's this: who we are may be pre-determined to a great extent, but the path we choose to follow can be our own choosing.

I once received a birthday card from my friend Sara that said 'put yourself first' on the front. I remember my initial reaction to reading those words. My inner voice said, 'That's a very selfish thing to do. I am not like that!' And then I rationalised it to myself by saying, 'Hold on, it's your birthday. You're allowed to put yourself first today!' (What a sad sack!)

As I sit here sharing this with you, I am hoping you can see how self-limiting my reaction was. How *dare* I make myself a priority? For many of us, putting ourselves last is a regular occurrence, isn't it? We sacrifice our needs for everyone else's. We wear the 'sacrificial lamb' tag as a badge of honour. Even leadership guru Simon Sinek says 'good leaders eat last'.[18]

I fundamentally disagree with him. The critical leadership lesson for me is one that separates unreasonably ambitious leaders from the rest, and it is this: there is no greater act of self-love and personal leadership than *taking care of yourself first*.

> **There is no greater act of self-love and personal leadership than taking care of yourself first.**

Who's twitching right now? Who is thinking I'm a self-focused twat?

But just think about this for a second. When you're on a plane and about to take off, the safety briefing instructs you to put your own mask on before attending to the needs of others. The reason is logical: you cannot possibly help anyone else if you can't breathe yourself.

It's the same with learning and evolving. The decisions we make as leaders as to how we spend our time and how we choose to invest our energy dictate what comes next. We should never allow our fears or the expectations of others to direct how far we travel in our own lives; how high the mountains are that we climb.

Unreasonably ambitious leaders have a clear line of sight to their goals and ambitions – even if they may seem wildly out of reach in the immediate future.

## TAKE BACK THE STEERING WHEEL

Nobel Peace Prize winner and social entrepreneur Muhammad Yunus has a wonderful way of putting it. He says, 'We are the pilots of this spaceship, planning our flight paths, not the passengers.'

He's right to urge us to take back the steering wheel and not neglect our future selves. But here lies the challenge: how do we care about the future self we haven't met yet?

Let's do a little self-experiment. I'd like you to try to imagine your life right now if you had made study and career choices based on the ideal life you envisaged for yourself early on.

What would you have learned? What skills would you have mastered? Where would you have chosen to live? Who would you have spent the most time with?

The extent to which you can feel psychologically connected to your future self will influence how well you are able to bring forward the shadow of the future.

There is one trait that pulses through the veins of every unreasonably ambitious leader: a voracious curiosity. This fuels a passion for lifelong learning and clear future-oriented decisions; and a steely motivation to shape their own destiny and channel it in the aspired direction.

As I am writing this, I can't help but conjure stereotypical images of the type of kid that sets up a lemonade stand on their front lawn to get some pocket money. We can infer that they are displaying early signs of entrepreneurial industriousness, an impressive work ethic and the building of strong financial acumen – think of the contrast between the main characters in Robert Kiyosaki's *Rich Dad Poor Dad* (what a great book!).[19] The book, first published in 1997, tells the story of a boy with two fathers, one rich and one poor, to help develop a mind-set and the financial knowledge to build a life of wealth and freedom.

What's interesting is that a wealth mindset is purported to be a set of beliefs, habits and behaviours that separates the wealthy from the rest. Kiyosaki says, 'A wealth mindset will guide you to make the most of the money you have.'

If you think about this more broadly, Kiyosaki's rich dad character has what we know in positive psychology as an abundant mentality. This mentality is characterised as opting to live life to the full, exuding happiness, being generous by nature, and being creative and inspirational. Those with an abundant frame take full advantage of opportunities that come their way, along with memorable experiences. As the famous quote from Bob Ross, American painter and TV personality, suggests: 'The secret to having it all is believing you already do.'

In contrast, the poor dad persona has a mindset of scarcity, feeling like he never has enough. People with this 'glass half empty' mentality tend to experience more anxiety. They have a singular focus on what is missing from their lives: not having enough, not being enough.

In the world of high-stakes business and leadership performance, having an abundant mindset has been scientifically proven to separate winners from losers at work, and allow greater fulfilment in life – because *what you think, you are*.[20] I'll expand on this in chapter 20.

## BECOME THE ENTREPRENEUR OF YOUR OWN LIFE

I've met many former lemonade stand kids as adults, and I've found their stories follow a similar thread of early ingenuity, bold curiosity and a willingness to invest their time and energy into creating a better life for themselves. From a banker who sold newspapers on his pushbike, to a paraplegic who became a millionaire by selling pens on the street, and a venture capitalist who paid his way through law school by posing nude for art classes and selling his neat lecture notes to other students – the gene is seemingly inbuilt, and kicks off when they're young. The drive to take risks and develop themselves no matter how frightening it may feel is just a natural part of their modus operandi. It's organic and unconscious. (I mean, would you pose nude in front of a class of art students?)

Whether you feel you are naturally wired this way or not, your journey to becoming an unreasonably ambitious leader starts with a conscious and intentional commitment to becoming the entrepreneur of your own life.

There are many new frontiers in life. A frontier is 'any boundary between where we feel comfortable and where we don't'.[21] Being able to realise dreams that may seem unfathomable means stepping boldly towards the infinite number of frontiers, because 'you have to stand at the edge of these wild places if you want to create something new'.[22]

Here are some questions to ask yourself.

## Reflection

- Which new frontiers do you have to step towards to live your best life? To do your best work?

- Are you prepared to put in the time and effort required to make your life dreams a reality?

- In which areas of your life do you need to invest to accelerate your readiness to live the life you want?

- Are you willing to stop doing those things that could block you from evolving your desired life?

- Are you brave enough to feel the fear and do it anyway?

- What are you prepared to give up to get there?

Just as the oak tree has deep roots grounding it to the earth, so does a strong sense of self bind us to the truth of who we are and help us to stay on course, no matter how windy the conditions.

We are almost ready to move to the next part of the book, but before we do, I'd like to encourage you to review what you've learned about yourself from part II. This will help you clarify your values and purpose, and fuel your hunger for growth. It is these core elements that create the sturdiest platform to withstand any storm. Building these are *prerequisites* for what comes next.

Here's another way to think about it. Imagine that you have climbed up a trapeze and you are ready to jump. Knowing yourself, what you stand for and that you are at the helm of your own future forms a *psychological safety net*. It's flexible yet strong and there to catch you – should you need it. Knowing it's there will fuel your willingness to leap into what comes next. It will motivate you to do the work to activate your gifts, have courage to pursue them and learn the skills to play an infinite game in life.[23]

To be a finite player in life is to accept the role life gives you and play by established rules in an effort to win. Finite players struggle with unpredictability, uncertainty and not knowing. These are the leaders who have an 'if it ain't broke don't fix it' attitude, and who struggle to make sense of the new complexity of business.

Conversely, the infinite player challenges prescribed roles and bends the rules – not to win the game, but for the simple joy of playing. For infinite players, uncertainty is a gift that presents a realm of opportunity. Elon Musk, Tesla and SpaceX founder, is an unreasonably ambitious leader who continues to play the infinite game with his limitless, unorthodox approach to problem-solving and belief in the impossible.

> The infinite player challenges prescribed roles and bends the rules – not to win the game, but for the simple joy of playing.

## Reflection

- Which player do you choose to be?
- What are the mantras you live by?
- What mindset do you bring to life and work?

# PART III

# MIND

# SET

The mind is a powerful force. It can enslave
us or empower us. It can plunge us into the depths
of misery or take us to the heights of ecstasy.
Learn to use the power wisely.

– DAVID CUSCHIERI

It's a well-known fact that we only use about 40 per cent of our brain power. The quest to unlock the other 60 per cent has become like the search for the holy grail. It's one of our most highly sought-after commodities, and there are some who would try just about anything to get access to it.

From elite military personnel and crazy-arse tech heads to game-changing trailblazers, these folks are hacking their minds in an effort to boost their ability to solve critical challenges and outperform the competition. The bottom line is, there is a war raging in the world of work, and to keep up requires a complete rethinking of human possibility.

In their book *Stealing Fire*, Steven Kotler and Jamie Wheal discuss exploring altered states of consciousness via the use of LSD micro-dosing, also known as 'ecstatic technologies', to unlock human potential, creativity and peak performance.[24] They describe it as 'trying to get into flow which is that ultimate state of consciousness where we feel our best and perform our best' (in case you're wondering, I am not endorsing this; but it certainly provides us with some interesting food for thought!).

In just a minute we will go deep into learning about how to cultivate and sustain a mindset of unreasonable ambition *without* having to be in an altered state. In the pages that follow I will present you with eight adaptive challenges to disrupt your thinking and activate a mental revolution. These adaptive challenges are designed to stretch your current ways of being and thinking. Together we'll blow up any old records you've been playing in your head on repeat, rewire obsolete programming and bury any entrenched beliefs that are holding you back from realising your full potential.

If you're feeling apprehensive, you should be. Accepting the challenge of a mental reboot is hard work. It requires the heavy lifting of mindset shift and leadership transformation. But we are going to do this the healthy way, drug free, without a rainbow-haired naked person in sight. I promise!

I've spent the last 20 years working with modern-day revolutionaries to help them get into a sustained and optimal state of flow. Armed with some easy-to-apply skills and psychological know-how, you too will be able to maintain positive mental mojo and catapult your own performance when it matters the most.

And by the way, it was in this mindset that coders built the internet and video gamers built the gaming industry. Have I got your attention?

Before we get into it, I have two very important questions to ask you:

1.  Do you believe you have within you the ability to realise your wildest dreams beyond measure?
2.  Do you believe that you are already hardwired for agility and speed?

If your answer is *yes*, stay with me and read on.

If your answer is *no*, read on anyway. I might just change your mind.

# CHALLENGE 1

# EMBRACING THE SUCK

**Which is more real, when you face reality, or when reality faces you?**

**– ANTHONY LICCIONE**

There is a movie moment that has stayed with me forever. It takes place in the 1992 blockbuster *The Power of One*. It's based on Bryce Courtenay's novel about a young English-speaking South African boy, Peekay, raised under apartheid, whose peaceful life is turned upside down when he is sent to a conservative Afrikaans boarding school while his mother recovers from a nervous breakdown.

Perhaps you've heard of it?

There is one scene in which Morgan Freeman, playing the boy's boxing coach, is looking at a 'mighty' waterfall with young Peekay, contemplating the mysteries of life. Peekay had gone through so many testing times, and like many of us in those moments was wondering what it all meant and why it was happening to him. His coach turned to him and said, 'Peekay, all the answers to life's great questions can be found in nature.'

I believe in that. We can learn so much about how our minds work from nature and the animal kingdom.

There is no doubt that, in the wild, life decisions are a lot more cut and dry. Think about what happens to a baby giraffe when it's born. The first thing the mother does when she sees her newborn baby is kick it with her hoof! I am not talking a gentle little tap, but successive, furious smacks. Why does she kick her baby so hard? It sounds extreme, doesn't it?

The learning for us here is that life in the wild is dangerous. To survive, the baby giraffe needs to get moving immediately! Unexpected things happen all the time that can have dire consequences, particularly in a perilous savannah habitat.

The irony is that modern-day life could be described in the same way. Yet the difference between giraffes and humans is that giraffes' minds are not full of noise and fear that clouds judgement. Decisions are purely instinctive – it's about survival of the fittest, which keeps things very simple. Get moving or get eaten!

As humans, we often ignore the cues of impending change, don't we? Life provides us with first alerts much like the mother giraffe's kick, trying to get us ready for pre-emptive action before we find ourselves in turmoil.

But we don't act on the signals. We rationalise them. We fear them. We ignore them. We stick our heads in the sand, choosing comfort over courage; stability over upheaval.

We have all been asked the following question by someone who is preparing us to receive information they believe may upset us: 'Do you want the good news, or the bad news?' Most people will request the good news first, because they fear having to deal with the bad news.

To become unreasonably ambitious means not viewing news as bad or good, but simply as news to be digested and actioned. It's a mindset of viewing any news or feedback as an opportunity to be seized to amplify our own growth and evolution. To do so requires us to respond quickly to first alerts before fear takes over. It's also about cultivating a mindset where changes are interpreted as growth opportunities, not as threats to be avoided.

The unreasonably ambitious reframe their innate fear response in favour of *facing reality as it is, not as they wish it to be* – and just get on with it.

Much like the baby giraffe, building our capability as unreasonably ambitious leaders to learn from our experiences at an accelerated rate will increase our ability to adapt faster to the ever-changing world that surrounds us.

Challenge 1: embracing the suck focuses on building the perspective and mental stamina to tackle the things you fear the most, enabling you to leverage the greatest opportunities for your own exponential growth.

I am about to lay down the gauntlet and dare you to shake life by the shoulders and welcome all the seasons into your life – winter, spring, summer and autumn. Because, let's face it, we are at a point in our evolution where life (much like the mother giraffe) is kicking us, compelling us to adapt our mindsets so we can thrive.

It's up to you. The decision to live your best life is in your hands. Here are your two options:

1. Stand still and become extinct, like the dodo bird.
2. Get moving and thrive.

If you chose option number 2, read on. You are ready for the adventure that lies ahead. You are ready to embrace the suck.

# CHAPTER 9

# CONFRONTING TRUTH HEAD-ON

It does not do to dwell on dreams and forget to live.

– JK ROWLING

Being able to step into any of life's challenges with strength and courage requires us to go in with eyes wide open and face the truth. Research into what makes certain people the happiest on the planet reveals *not* that they are lunatics, but that they embrace often harsh realities; that they have built the skills to work through difficulties to get to the other side more quickly than most.

Have you noticed how many management consultants have been contracted into organisations to help them manage change? Over the last 20 years, big human capital firms have made millions offering change management courses and methodologies to support humans at work to deal with the reality of simply being human. I've noticed many organisations adopting Elisabeth Kübler-Ross's five stages of grieving model to navigate work-related changes, which gives me pause. Don't get me wrong, it's a clever model – but I wonder, is it really the most relevant perspective we can come up with to help workers shift their reactions to change at work?

As an organisational psychologist, I admit I see a loose connection between metaphoric death and dealing with loss in the workplace. Yet the flaw is in the premise of these services. If change is a natural and constant part of life, what are we *really* managing? Can we truly manage something that we have zero control over, like dying?

Standing on the sidelines, seeing organisations perplexed as to why they can't get traction on their change programs, is frustrating to me. Garden variety change management programs are based on a fundamental psychological flaw in how change is framed. The truth is that *we cannot control all changes that happen to us* in our lives; but that doesn't mean we can't be better prepared (we'll discuss this in more detail in challenge 5: seeing the future).

**Learning how to move with change is an enhanced psychological state of being.**

After all, that's what change is, right? The experience of something new, and accepting that things aren't the way they used to be. What we can do is learn to move with it. Learning how to *move with change* is an enhanced psychological state of being where a person makes an intentional choice in that moment of how they are going to interpret and process change.

## GET OVER IT AND MOVE ON

Unreasonably ambitious leaders recognise what they are up against and tend to move through the cycles of change a lot faster than others. They embrace the suck of a situation, get over it quickly and move to action (or reinvention, in some cases). Part of the skill lies in being able to self-diagnose where they are at, and then figure out what they need to do to move through to a healthy, high-functioning state quickly and with minimal scarring.

Think about Mr Titan, who we met in the preface of this book. The economic conditions he was facing were grim. Yet he managed to work through his emotions swiftly to get into a state of inspired creativity, while Mr Magnate collapsed into a heap. The upshot? When they were tested, Mr Titan flourished while Mr Magnate floundered.

I have so much respect for the Chinese enlightened way of looking at change. Their word for crisis, *weiji*, is a combination of symbols that represent both danger and opportunity. This translation has been blown up as 'rubbish' recently, but I still believe that a crisis can also present an opportunity not to be wasted. Crisis can be a catalyst for incredible momentum, meaningful progress and evolution.

If you trace the history of some of our world's cult classic innovations, such as Heinz condensed tomato soup and McDonald's, many were borne during eras of destitution and scarcity rather than abundance and happy times.

I worked with a high-profile northern goldfields nickel operation during some major bust years. Management had to slash 300 jobs as part of a company-wide cost reduction exercise. The decision was propelled by a plunge in the price of steelmaking as a commodity, which had already made many of Western Australia's once profitable nickel operations unviable.

This stark economic reality coupled with bad safety performance compelled the organisation's leadership team to make a serious commitment to rebuild the operation with a long-term vision in mind: to become the front end of a great nickel operation. But it would come at a cost.

The turnaround strategy was three-fold:

1.  Recalibrate the business with a focus on making the mine site a safe place to work.
2.  Move to a new operating model.
3.  Set a new strategic direction for the way forward.

To put this into perspective, these decisions represented a loss of about 6 per cent of the company's workforce. I had been hired with the ambitious mandate to help return the mine to full productivity within nine months, and heal the workforce after large-scale downsizing (not done well!). The organisation ended up achieving its aims. It was sold off and incorporated as part of a new mining company several years later.

I've worked with hundreds of leadership teams over the past 20 years, but this one was a standout. The leaders were the primary drivers of the positive outcomes achieved.

What set them apart was their unyielding commitment to confront the truth and not shield their people from it. Their willingness to have raw and unfiltered discussions often placed these leaders in the firing line, barraged by the artillery of scared and angry humans clawing for clarity and certainty.

But in the crisis, the leaders were able to maintain a view of the upside. They saw the downturn not as a tragedy but as valuable time to recalibrate the operation and recreate a future with employees driving its resurrection.

I will never forget standing alongside the senior leadership team in high-vis gear battling oppressive 45-degree heat and very basic conditions, presenting the 'brutal truth' to groups of 50 employees at a time. At first, the vibe in the room was hostile, mistrustful and tense. Faces were scowled and arms were crossed; perspiration dripped down onto their collars. I could hear the crowd muttering successive expletives. They didn't hold back.

And then something extraordinary happened. The tide turned. The mood changed. The leaders went from dodging bullets and criticism, judgement and blame to witnessing tears, relief and even laughter. The decision to be transparent at all costs and provide surviving employees with a forum to air their true feelings and be supported in looking towards an unknown future accelerated the healing process. It created deeper connections and purpose within the team, and greater trust of the organisation.

The mine was back running on full throttle within nine months.

So, let's break down the magic that happened here:

· Making the decision to lead with the 'brutal truth' created the conditions for clarity and honesty.
· Having the courage to embrace the suck and work through the implications of their reality sped up the healing process for the remaining workforce.
· Stepping into and working through reactions together fast-tracked the team's collective ability to move through the cycle of change to a more productive mindset and get on with it.
· Creating space for unfiltered conversation forced a focus on the silver lining: the opportunity to build a more exciting and sustainable future for the organisation long term.

So, what's the moral of the story? Building your mindset to handle adverse situations starts with *not running from them*. At no point in working with this leadership team did anyone pull their feet off the accelerator as we drove towards a viable end game. Unreasonable ambition means choosing to put yourself into the line of fire, knowing you have what it takes to tackle the tough stuff no matter what.

I'm making it sound easy, I know (I can assure you it isn't). Like learning any new habit or skill, it takes commitment and practice to nail it. Learning how to capitalise on any anxiety or stress that comes from choosing to stand in the eye of the storm starts with a decision to confront it head-on.

In the next chapter we'll talk about the benefits of making friends with your stress, harnessing it for good.

## Reflection

- Think about a situation that really stressed you out, that sparked creative adaptation and realised positive returns. Remember the moment when you flipped from tension to achievement. Replay it for a moment. What did it feel like? How can you recreate this?

- What is your default approach when you have to deliver bad news? Do you avoid the conversation, stall and side-step, or dive straight in and deliver it? Knowing how you naturally resolve conflict is a good indication of how comfortable you are keeping it real and leading others through tough times.

- Do you take time to diagnose your own emotional reactions to people and situations? The more you can lift your unconscious mind into full-frontal conscious awareness the faster you will move through stress.

# CHAPTER 10

# MAKING FRIENDS WITH STRESS

Somehow our devils are never quite what
we expect when we meet them face to face.

– NELSON DeMILLE

I have always loved to run. I really got into it when I started working in a very fast-paced corporate career that saw me pulling all-nighters and living off gallons of insipid Starbucks coffee that looked like dirty dishwater.

From the outside in, many would have described my life as stressful. Yes, my life *was* frenetic, yet regular running was the one thing I was able to maintain no matter how mentally exhausted I was. Anyone who is a runner knows that magic moment when the endorphins kick in, sending your body awash with elevated feelings of joy and pleasure – just at the point where you feel like you can't take another step. It's called a runner's high. When these chemicals are released into my brain, I am able to endure longer runs without quitting or feeling any physical pain. I am able to push through to get to the end.

## NOT ALL STRESS IS CREATED EQUAL

I know it sounds counterintuitive, but in psychology we know that a little bit of stress or fear can incite higher performance levels. And that is exactly what happens to leaders who are unreasonably ambitious. Channelling my stress hormones through running has always helped me to keep a clear head and stay focused, even during periods of work overload. It boosts my mental acuity, supercharges my decision-making and leads to better outcomes. It's like that for anyone who can harness their stress energy to turn a potential negative feeling into a positive outcome.

So, why is it that stress gets such a bad rap? It's because it is often confused with *distress* or *burnout*. Burnout is the dark side of stress at work. It's defined by the World Health Organization (WHO) as 'a syndrome conceptualised as resulting from chronic workplace stress that has not been successfully managed'.[25] The WHO characterises it by three dimensions:

1. feelings of energy depletion or exhaustion
2. increased mental distance from one's job, or feelings of negativism or cynicism related to one's job
3. reduced professional efficacy.

Your approach to managing your workload, and the cultural expectations placed on you at work about accepted levels of work, play a huge part in building your habits around this.

In contrast, 'happy' stress, also known as *eustress*, is positive stress brought on by exciting or stimulating events. It causes a chemical response in the body akin to the feeling of euphoria.

> **'Happy' stress, also known as eustress, is positive stress brought on by exciting or stimulating events.**

Sounds pretty good right? It is, particularly if you can tap into it!

The following figure shows how it all works.

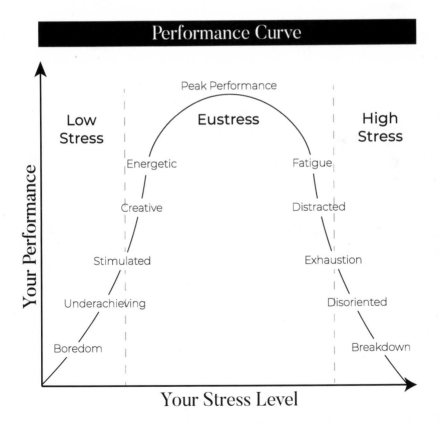

## Performance Curve

## CAPITALISING ON STRESS ENERGY

I met my university friend, Lynn, when we were both studying psychology. I've heard it said that some people become psychologists to sort out their own issues, and in Lynn's case this was probably true.

Lynn is one of the messiest and most disorganised people I have ever met. Back then she smoked way too much weed and walked around effing and blinding. She would show up to class late and pull out her dog-eared notebooks, stained with coffee and stinking of cigarettes. She would borrow my lecture notes because they were 'neater than hers' (she couldn't read hers most of the time).

Lynn was a walking disaster. She was also the brightest student in our class, and it annoyed the hell out of me!

When exam time came around, Lynn would show up to Winthrop Hall (it's kind of like Western Australia's rendition of Hogwarts) a few minutes before start time. Most days she had forgotten her pen and asked to borrow mine. She always looked disheveled, like she had just rolled out of bed – which she usually had, being an all-nighter devotee.

And then the unthinkable would happen. Lynn would blitz her exams, getting near-perfect scores and graduating top of our psychology class. I never understood it!

There I would be, studying for weeks on end, preparing answers to any questions I might get asked, bringing a whole bag of Bic pens just in case they ran out of ink, and Lynn graduated cum laude leaving me shaking my head in disbelief.

Most of us have known someone like Lynn.

The important lesson here is that the Lynns of this world do not necessarily have more special gifts – but they do know how to make their stress work them. Lynn didn't run away from stress; she hugged it tight.

## KNOWING WHEN YOU'RE IN THE ZONE

I recall Lynn spoke a lot about circadian rhythms. At the time I didn't really get what she was on about. I thought she was a bit of a fruit loop (you know, colourful and a bit zany).

Since then, I have realised just how clever Lynn really was.

You see, Lynn was most mentally alert and productive at night. That's why she pulled all-nighters. I, on the other hand, have always been a morning lark. Even now I avoid evening networking events because I am a walking corpse by around 8.30 pm; I start slurring my words and have to actively manage myself so my head doesn't drop into my soup bowl!

Lynn's wisdom was in recognising the times when she was firing on all cylinders. She gave herself the edge by only working during periods of high mental alertness. She replaced potential stress with being *in flow*. This amplified her productivity, leaving the rest of us trailing in her wake.

At the 2021 Olympics, Australian beach volleyball champion Natalie Cook said, 'We were taught 21 years ago that the butterflies were going to be there. Get your butterflies into formation, so they can fly you over the net to the gold medal.' I recall famous swimming icon Dawn Fraser saying the very same thing decades earlier.

The bottom line? People with unreasonable ambition don't let stress level them. They accept that it is a natural part of life. They don't try to get rid of it entirely, but learn to channel it to fuel superior performance. They find ways to *make stress work for them*.

**People with unreasonable ambition don't let stress level them.**

You may be wondering what happened to Lynn. Did she go on to win a Fulbright scholarship to Harvard? Did she go into medicine and become a brain surgeon?

She probably could have. Last time I heard from Lynn she was pregnant and living in a hippy commune in Mackay, Queensland with her partner, a heavily bearded Greenpeace activist, and their pit bull terrier.

Yes, Lynn was able to harness her eustress to create extraordinary outcomes. Yes, she was able to maximise her natural operating rhythms to exploit her cognitive capacity in the moment.

However, while Lynn had the DNA of an unreasonably ambitious person, she did not match it with the same levels of discipline to *execute* and *do something with her potential*. She did not choose this path.

*Unreasonably ambitious* leaders exploit all their gifts (albeit not necessarily all at the same time) to make magic happen. We'll learn more about execution in challenge 6: supercharging your productivity.

For now, repeat after me: *Stress is my friend. Stress is my friend. Stress is my friend.*

Now, let's move on to pain.

## Reflection

· How can you befriend your stress?

· Think about current stressors in your life and think about your level of control. What is in your control and what is out of your control? Make a list and here is a tip – your only focus is on working through what you have control over and making different decisions about how to manage it e.g. your current work situation is causing you anxiety and you have lost your passion for the role. You are making a choice to stay there. Proactively start exploring new opportunities to move on and get ready for departure. It's the same for relationships – you can say no to people in your life who are toxic or creating anxiety for you. Make a decision to move away from them or restrict the interactions with them.

# CHAPTER 11

# LEARNING TO LOVE PAIN

Pain is temporary. It may last a minute, or an hour, or a day, or a year, but eventually it will subside and something else will take its place. If I quit, however, it lasts forever.

– LANCE ARMSTRONG

Several years ago, a story hit the headlines about the questionable spending habits of younger Australians. The story claimed that many of them were still living at home well into their late 20s and mid-30s. Australian Bureau of Statistics figures showed 25- to 34-year-olds were the only ten-year age bracket to have gone backwards in income over two years, while household income had flatlined since 2009.[26] The most memorable example given of the overspending habit was the trend of paying $20 per serve for smashed avocado on toast for breakfast, versus saving money to buy a home. The data showcased how this generation was literally 'out to lunch' in terms of what it takes to get ahead financially.

At the time, I found the media on this thought-provoking. Even now, observing the behaviours of people around me, it seems as if many would do just about anything to escape the pain of everyday living. How is it that even payment options have become 'frictionless' in an effort for us not to experience the anguish of handing over our hard-earned cash?

Yet, that pain is exactly what we need to be experiencing.

Think about what the inability to deal with pain has done to the smashed avocado generation. Could it be that helicopter parenting (parents who hover and supervise every aspect of their children's lives), easy accessibility of online goods and services and painless spending are making us soft and less resilient?

Life is a series of ups and downs. As the saying goes, 'it takes rain and sunshine to make a rainbow'. Trying to eliminate the pain of life could actually be *hurting us more*.

## PAIN IS OUR TEACHER

As a researcher I have spent quite a bit of time in hospital wards. On one such occasion, I was in the ICU ward at Sir Charles Gairdner Hospital in Western Australia. I was there to evaluate the impact of nursing staff stress on quality of patient care. There I was, day and night, taking saliva samples before and after 12- and eight-hour shifts to determine which working arrangements increased effectiveness, productivity and patient-related outcomes, and how they related to stress levels.

I met a beautiful little boy called Connor. He has been admitted with third-degree burns from boiling oil that had tipped onto him from a deep fryer in his home kitchen. What made this case so memorable for me was that Connor was born with a rare condition rendering him unable to feel physical pain. It's called congenital insensitivity to pain, or *congenital analgesia*. Kids like Connor who don't receive cues from their physical pain receptors have to cope with life in a very different way.

Think about it. Even a hot cup of coffee can be highly dangerous without the ability to experience the sensation of a burning tongue as you sip your boiling brew. As a result, children who are born with this condition have a significantly reduced life expectancy.

Meeting Connor and realising he was living on borrowed time was heart-wrenching for a highly sensitive person like me, and yet I learned an important life lesson that I am grateful for: *pain and discomfort play a critical role in our evolution.* Pain enables us to live longer and teaches us to bloom.

To build an unreasonably ambitious mindset requires us to stop trying so hard to avoid the inevitable pain in life, and instead learn to deal with it – knowing that we can handle more than we imagine.

**To build an *unreasonably ambitious mindset* requires us to stop trying so hard to avoid the inevitable pain in life, and instead learn to deal with it.**

There's a wonderful passage in the Bible that speaks to this. It serves as a very powerful reminder for us all, whether we believe in God or not. 1 Corinthians 10:13 teaches: 'God won't give you more than you can handle.' (Stay with me on this.) This verse reminds us that 'no temptation has overtaken you that is not common to man. God is faithful, and He will not let you be tempted beyond your ability, but with the temptation. He will provide the way of escape, that you may be able to endure it.'

## WALKING THROUGH FIRE

I have noticed that leaders with unreasonable ambition step into pain and skip quickly through it.

Many years ago, I took part in a fire-walking activity as part of a Tony Robbins personal transformation program in Las Vegas. The thought of walking over hot coals even just for a few seconds was terrifying. And yet here we were, one by one, skipping over them as if they were made of cool marble. We had faces of sheer terror at the start, replaced with starry jubilation as we jumped off the last glowing embers to land on the ground.

Unreasonably ambitious leaders can walk over fire to build mental toughness. They don't just endure it; they are motivated by it.

**Unreasonably ambitious leaders can walk over fire to build mental toughness. They don't just endure it; they are motivated by it.**

In truth, there is no escaping pain in life. Learning to lean into that pain is a mammoth leap into our untapped potential and successful adaptation to life.

It's as simple as that.

Now let's explore the power of owning your emotions.

## Reflection

- What lengths do you go to to avoid experiencing pain or discomfort?

- When have you surprised yourself by confronting and overcoming your initial fears?

- Is there a time when stepping into a frightening situation has grown your feelings of confidence and self-worth, leading to you seizing bigger opportunities later down the track?

# CHAPTER 12

# GETTING IN TOUCH WITH YOUR FEELINGS

If you don't have empathy for yourself,
you can't give it to others.

– MICHAEL VENTURA

Hard-arse leadership is out. Getting in touch with your feelings is in.

Just as escaping pain is not an option for leaders who want to successfully navigate an uncertain future, neither is running away from emotions.

In a world that is becoming increasingly digitised and automated, the power of feelings and empathy are viewed as top commodities in the world of work. It's what differentiates us from machines and gives us the ability to engage people's hearts and minds, especially during times of constant change.

The unreasonably ambitious leader's skill lies in being able to see the world through the eyes of another; in feeling perfectly comfortable sitting with emotions and helping others work through theirs.

Unfortunately, this skill is rarely seen.

I have run thousands of workshops over the years to upskill leaders in having difficult conversations and resolving mounting tensions and conflict. There is one role-play I facilitate where I ask participants to play a highly reactive person (the 'Client') who has emotional outbursts, while the other person tries to be the 'Coach' and work them through the presenting issue.

Nine times out of ten, the role-play is acted out in the same way. The Coach to the highly emotional Client shuts down in the face of an intense reaction, immobilised by fear, uncomfortable with the expressed emotion. What happens next is predictable – the Coach tries to steer the Client to the *doing*, to problem-solving. They ignore the emotions of the person sitting before them, preferring to move into 'stealth' mode and find solutions. Meanwhile, the Client sits before them, crying, angry, turning red with embarrassment, shaking with anxiety or scratching their head in despair.

You get the gist.

The other common reaction is to 'freeze them out' (that's my technical term for it). This is where the Coach becomes stern and even cold, trying to subdue the intensity of the interaction and deal with their own discomfort by just getting on with it. They pretend to be oblivious to the pain of the person screaming for acknowledgement. (It's actually quite hard to watch!)

As an observer, it's difficult to fathom how the Coach could be so unaware of the train wreck they are veering towards; that a human caboose is about to burst into flames, and they could have stopped it.

Yet it happens, time and time again. Instead of owning their own emotions and acknowledging those of the Client, the Coach makes a run for the hills when emotions show up to the party.

So where does this leave us?

Our future depends on leaders' ability to connect more deeply with their people; to tune in to the feelings of the person behind the professional. Long-term business sustainability rests on our ability as unreasonably ambitious leaders to speak to both the hearts and minds of our people (and souls – but I don't want to get too 'out there' with you just yet).

It's the hardest work you will ever have to do in your life. That's why not everyone is cut out for it.

So, if you have made the decision to take up the leadership mantle, you'd better be prepared for what's to come.

*There is nothing soft about leading people.*

**There is nothing soft about leading people.**

## THE BUSINESS CASE FOR EMOTIONS

The clock is ticking.

We are in the era of a revolution; a revolution of human relationships. Never before have we lived in a world so divided, pushing us all further and further apart from each other in life and at work. Empathy is a necessary skill to begin bringing us all closer together, so we can solve for the future and create the world we want to live in.

With over one-third (35 per cent) of the skills considered 'important' in today's workforce different to those of five years ago, it becomes paramount for leaders to be able to read the thoughts and motivations of their team members and be equipped to guide them through the rapid pace of change.[27]

Why? Because empathic leaders can respond more quickly and at scale to stakeholder needs, collaborate more successfully and achieve far greater results than one person or one team could achieve on their own.[28]

Empathy is not about being nice; it's about being human. It's what differentiates us from robots.

Consider this insight: 'Silicon Valley's biggest failing is not poor marketing of its products, or follow-through on promises, but, rather, the distinct lack of empathy for those whose lives are disturbed by its technological wizardry'.[29]

A renewed focus on empowering and engaging people and customers and putting humanity centre stage will enable us to address the growing empathy gap and successfully topple the threat of business extinction.

Empathy makes perfect business sense.

A mind-blowing example of this in practice is in Satya Nadella's impressive turnaround of Microsoft, a feat that has put the world on notice. Nadella lifted the company to around 84 per cent growth in the stock price over the last three years. He did it by moving leaders to a growth mindset in which empathy – being able to 'walk a mile in someone else's shoes' – was a key competitive differentiator. According to Nadella, 'Empathy is the exclusive human quality that no machine or technology application can rival.'[30]

## BUT WHAT EXACTLY IS EMPATHY?

Empathy is the ability to share and understand others' emotions – not to be confused with sympathy, which is having feelings of pity or sorrow for someone else's misfortune. Empathy enables you to connect with others and offer solutions. Sympathy usually results in a person taking on the emotions of others to the point where they are unable to offer constructive support or suffer with the person needing help. The sympathetic person is the one who cries when you cry, and blows their nose at the same time.

I often ask my clients which they think is more effective – a senior human resources professional who is highly emotive and a feeling person, or one who is more data-rational and bases decisions on facts?

The answer is usually the former.

To make good people decisions, it's wiser to be someone who is empathic but still able to maintain objectivity; someone who doesn't get caught in the spiral of presenting emotions, but who remains on the outer edge, providing support.

An unreasonably ambitious leader has a healthy relationship with all human emotions and is not afraid to feel them all.

---

**An unreasonably ambitious leader has a healthy relationship with all human emotions and is not afraid to feel them all.**

---

They give themselves and others *permission to feel*.

Rumi's 'The Guest House' is one of my favourite poems. I recommend looking it up if you are not familiar with it. Rumi expresses the desire for human beings to get to a place where they see the experiencing of the kaleidoscope of human emotions as gifts to be welcomed and celebrated.

In an evolved society, to feel does not require us to ask permission.

## Reflection

- Think about the decisions you make at work. Do you tend to balance compassion with realism or favour relationships over achieving results? Think about your natural inclination. Is there a way to better balance the scales in priorities that may be seemingly in competition with each other?

- How do you respond to emotions? Are you comfortable experiencing them all or do you try to shut off parts of yourself to cope better?

- How are you creating space to process any negative emotions to get your mindset into a more productive space?

# CHALLENGE 2

# NAVIGATING THE STORM

The cyclone derives its power from a calm center.
So does a person.

– NORMAN VINCENT PEALE

I believe that life is a series of spiritual tests, and some of us are tested more than others. I don't know why this is, but it's something I have noticed. And, given my own life story, I am probably one of those people who has been incessantly tested – whether I like it or not!

Here is what I have learned: how we respond in those moments defines us. It can even set us on a new path to a more evolved and better version of ourselves. At the time these tests can be painful, gruelling, tortuous even, but when we get to the other side we are forever altered – *for the better*.

I once had an experience that literally dropped me to my knees. If you've read Elizabeth Gilbert's memoir *Eat, Pray, Love*, you may recall the famous opening scene. It's 3 am and Gilbert is sobbing on the bathroom floor. She's in her 30s with a husband and a house. She and her husband are trying for a baby – and she doesn't want any of it. She is literally levelled with despair and grief at the realisation of this inconvenient truth, because she knows; she knows she must take action.

I had an experience just like that, where I was reduced to my knees in a blubbering mess on my front lawn. I had pioneered a new leadership program, Trail-Blazer, for trail-blazing women at work. Based on solid psychological building blocks and years of experience in transformative change, the program was considered groundbreaking. I even won an award for it a few years later.

I'd gotten sick of seeing women-only programs that failed to give people what they needed to shift the dial. These programs were superficial and token at best. I wanted to put the power back into women's hands so they could take charge of their destiny, and become confident risk-takers in their careers.

So, this program was a no-brainer, right? I mean, what could possibly go wrong?

It turned out to be by far the hardest program I have ever had to get off the ground, during my entire working career. As I went out to market, I was stunned at what I experienced. I discovered that few organisations would invest in a leadership program that was unique to and designed exclusively for women. This floored me, given the uncontested business case linking accelerated bottom-line returns with increased diversity at work.

The preference was for decision-makers to tick the proverbial 'gender' box by paying for subscriptions to send their female leaders to networking booze-ups, so they could swing around on poles and eat fairy-floss rather than invest in real change (I am not making this up!).

Regardless, the first year of the program got off to a great start. We had 12 participants ready to kick major life and work goals. Then, in the second year, we hit some *huge* roadblocks. After months of hustling (that's how it felt), trying to convince leaders that supporting a women's-only acceleration program was important, we finally had the ten participants I needed to run it.

And then I hit the next obstacle: my business partner had a change of heart about co-leading the program, opting to 'become a humanitarian'. Don't get me wrong, she was there physically – but mentally she had checked out, leaving me feeling alone in my passion and drive to deliver a knockout experience for our clients. It was a struggle for me to stay motivated and drag her to the end when I knew her heart wasn't in it. However, I dusted myself off and, undeterred, prepared to soldier on.

And then I hit the scariest obstacle of all. We were due to kick off the program in one week when I received a call that changed everything. Our main corporate sponsor, a large multinational building company, was pulling four women from the program. The company was experiencing financial challenges and could no longer make the investment.

I was already running the program at break-even. Without the sponsor's support, it would fold. After all the hard slog, the program would disappear like a puff of smoke. Just like that!

I remember the moment vividly. I had the phone in my hands, I felt my knees give way and I collapsed. I sobbed, I yelled, I cursed. My body shook with anxiety. (It was my *Eat, Pray, Love* moment!)

I had been fighting for months to keep the program alive. It meant something to me. I could hear the naysayers' voices, telling me I was playing a fool's game; that no-one cared about women's programs and I was wasting my time.

But it was the former graduates' voices whispering in my ear that reverberated more loudly. They had told me their lives had changed forever, and yet I was confronted with the possibility that the second program wasn't going to eventuate. That I had failed. That I was wrong.

And then something happened. I became completely calm.

I instinctively slowed down my breathing, consciously moved my mind into flow state and the ideas began flooding into my brain.

It was a 'limitless' moment, without the drugs.

I thought about all the wonderful women I had met while delivering motivational talks and presentations and remembered that my inbox was flooded with words of praise and gratitude.

*What if…?*

I jumped on the phone and started calling. Within 48 hours, six amazing female leaders had entered my life and joined the program.

We were ten, we were six, we were 12.

Unreasonably ambitious leaders do not only derive their success from the wins, but from *how they rise after they fall*. They move quickly to explore adjacent possibilities when things go awry, and put those possibilities into action.

In the following chapters we are going to be exploring the catalyst of fear and the power of calm as mighty forces to activate our unreasonable ambition when we need it the most.

# CHAPTER 13

# SEEING CLEARLY UNDERWATER

I must not fear. Fear is the mind-killer. Fear is the little death that brings total obliteration. I will face my fear. I will permit it to pass over me and through me. And when it has gone past, I will turn the inner eye to see its path. Where the fear has gone there will be nothing. Only I will remain.

– FRANK HERBERT, *DUNE*

I want to kick off this chapter with a true story and a warning.

If you are a person who is challenged by confronting harsh reality, *do not* read on. There is no judgement in my statement. Tackling the topic of death is confronting, and you must be ready to continue.

If you are still with me, read on. If you are not, skip to chapter 14.

A few years ago, the US Navy conducted some groundbreaking research to try to understand why many of their SEALs in training who drowned still had air in their tanks.

Yes, you heard me correctly: they died with air in their tanks.

So, what happened? It turned out the SEALs were instinctively pulling their regulators out of their mouths during underwater training.

It is completely normal for us as human beings to experience intense feelings of suffocation when our nose and mouth are covered. This leads to an overpowering impulse to uncover our nose and mouth. This is a good response under normal circumstances, but the wrong response under the unnatural conditions of scuba diving.

The point is, when you panic, you can't think clearly. You can't thrive if you are afraid, particularly in unknown environments where you don't have full control. In the case of the Navy SEALs, allowing their panic to take over led them to make fear-based decisions in an underwater environment, which ultimately led to their deaths.

When you are staring death in the face, being able to stay calm in the eye of the storm seems like an impossible ask. Or is it?

My Greek grandmother shared a story with me about her younger brother, Andreas. One of five children, he had left their island home of Patmos (that's in the Dodecanese Islands) in his early 20s to build an export business out of Africa into Europe. This was during World War II, and the plan was to keep the family afloat during this tough time.

The story goes that Andreas was wandering in the African jungle when he happened upon an enormous elephant. The elephant was aggressive (not how one normally thinks of elephants) and positioned his body to charge at Andreas. In that moment, my great uncle dropped to his knees, clutched the gold Saint Christopher medallion he wore around his neck and said, 'Saint Christopher, protect me!' The elephant apparently stopped in its tracks and lowered its head, while my great uncle lopped off one of its tusks.

Out of gratitude for being spared, Andreas donated the tusk to the Monastery of Saint John the Theologian on the island of Patmos where my family resided. I saw the tusk on a family holiday when I was a child – on display in one of the treasure cabinets for pilgrims to view when visiting the sacred site. (Disclaimer: I am not into killing animals or chopping off their tusks, but I get that this was a proud moment for my family back in the day!)

Since then, the bigger question I have pondered is this: how was Andreas able to flip himself into a state of calm and confront the elephant, even getting close enough to garner the 'trophy', without wobbling?

Research into tragedy survivors shows that when life and death is on the line, there are specific things survivors do that those who perish don't.[31] Survivors *adapt quickly to clear and present danger*; they get their brains into calm-down mode to better manage the precarious situation they find themselves in. A great example of this is explosive operators, whose heart rates have been shown to decelerate during the act of diffusing a bomb.

In the case of my great uncle Andreas, faith also played a huge part in his ability to step into the danger and stay calm, even in the face of his own mortality (we will talk more about faith in chapter 30).

You will often find that *unreasonably ambitious* leaders are able to maintain composure even in dangerous situations. There's an eerie calmness to how they hold themselves that's unnerving.

The secret lies in their ability to self-regulate faster, cool down any hot emotions and reinterpret what's happening to them in a more confident and positive way. In fact, many have even reported their greatest leadership moments as being when they had to navigate through their most harrowing life experiences.

*They don't get mad, they go quiet.* And that's what makes the difference.

## WHAT IT MEANS TO BE EMOTIONALLY AGILE

In high-risk or unfamiliar situations, our ability to make sense of what's going on, make good and fast decisions and execute quickly is instantly impaired *unless* we get into calm-down mode quickly and regain control of our emotions.

It's no mean feat, but learning how to short-circuit your neural hardwiring to stop yourself from reacting as if you need to run away from a stampede of elephants is paramount to a successful and fulfilling life. Dr Susan David calls this 'emotional agility', which she defines as 'approaching one's inner experiences mindfully and productively to better navigate the stresses and setbacks of our world'.[32]

Reacting from a foundation of emotional agility prevents you from becoming unstuck in situations that require you to get control of your emotions quickly before they take hold. It's what enables you to make better decisions in the heat of the moment.

Few of us will need to dodge an incensed African elephant in our lifetime. However, bolstering our ability to manage our thoughts and feelings when under fire is essential to business and life success.

The cornerstone of an unreasonably ambitious leader's power and skill is learning how to regulate distress, remain clear-headed and be fully in tune with all emotions (without drowning in them).

A widely held fallacy says that we become more resilient the more negative experiences we have in life. This is not true. *Repeated trauma does not build strength.* It's not a badge of courage to showcase how tough we really are.

What makes the difference is *how we process* challenging experiences. How we rewire our neural pathways as we rise out of the wreckage of traumatic events and experiences.

In the next chapter we are going to explore what psychologists call mental toughness, or 'grit'. It's how unreasonably ambitious leaders move their minds when their back is up against a wall, with no obvious way out.

It's how the unreasonably ambitious *consciously choose courage over fear.*

# Reflection

· Are there people or situations in your life that have caused you to feel emotionally stuck? What have you done to untangle yourself and move forward?

· How would you rate your own level of emotional agility? Are you able to roll with the punches of life, or do you have more of a catastrophic mindset?

· What opportunities have you seized or missed as a result of fear-based thinking?

# CHAPTER 14

# BRAVING THE WILDERNESS

I am about to undergo torture. How intense it will be I don't know yet. I am in the hands of experts, so I expect the worst... I am seated in a wooden chair in what I take to be an interrogation cell somewhere within the quarters of the revolutionary guard. I can't see a thing because I am wearing a blindfold... In such a situation, blind, lost, powerless – my fears are magnified... I imagine the hard barrel of a pistol pressed to the back of my head, then in that split second of life left to me I will mutter the words mother or father.

– DEAN SHARAFI, *THE UNWILLING REVOLUTIONARY: A TALE OF SOUL REDISCOVERY*

This is not an excerpt from a fictious tale.

I first met Amir (Dean) Sharafi, an Iranian-Australian executive, when he was leading the Operations Centre for Western Power Corporation.[33]

Sharafi's remit was to keep the lights on for all Western Australians on his grid. Think about the power in that: he had the authority to decide whether or not 2.3 million people had electricity. There's a kind of dramatic irony in that, given his story; where he came from (war-torn Iran); and what he has endured (being held hostage and tortured, not knowing whether he would live to see another day).

Uncovering Sharafi's story and his greatness took time. I was completely oblivious to the story he was holding back from sharing: a pivotal life experience that had transformed him from *ordinary* citizen to *extraordinary* leader. A story of unreasonable ambition that the world needed to hear. Like many reluctant leaders, Sharafi doesn't present as a typical hero. His incredible tale of bravery, mental fortitude and grit was hugely unexpected (shame on me!).

Medium in stature, quiet and humble with a nervous giggle, Sharafi doesn't take up much space or airtime. He is an active listener, a deep connector. He is present and unassuming, yet he has become one of the most powerful leaders in the Australian energy sector; he now works at the Australian Energy Market Operator (AEMO).[34]

Working with Sharafi was transformative for me as an executive high-performance coach and fellow human. He completely challenged my thinking about what brave leadership and mental toughness looks like in the flesh.

Mental toughness is the ability to manage and overcome doubts and circumstances that prevent you from excelling at something you set out to achieve. It's about three things: *self-belief*, *passion* and *perseverance*.

Sharafi's *self-belief* grew through his experiences into confidence and courage. His *passion* to make a difference as a leader propelled him into a coveted space in the energy sector. His *perseverance* and ability to bounce forward from adversity and channel his energy to push through difficulty with a positive world view has set him up for far-reaching impact.

## YOU'RE TOUGHER THAN YOU THINK

So, here's the deal: we are all tougher than we think. To unlock our inner well of toughness and grit, we must watch our prevailing tendency to underestimate our capacity to spring back from challenging situations and channel that energy to do something great.

Sharafi's story showcases that the real limits are those we place on ourselves. Human beings are hardwired to focus on the negative versus the positive. It's our brain's way of protecting us. But, clearly, that's not always serving us in everyday life.

Our neural programming can become an enemy to our adaptability – *if we don't learn how to rewire it.*

**Our neural programming can become an enemy to our adaptability – if we don't learn how to rewire it.**

I see it often: leaders who fall victim to a *maladaptive mindset.* Leadership teams that want to be able to withstand the toughest of workplace challenges, yet feel afraid and helpless.

And yet, as we learned in chapter 2, we have all been here before. Like Sharafi, we all have a story to tell. Everyone has experienced trials and tribulations in life, yet we forget too easily what we have overcome; how we have triumphed over adversity; the capabilities we have already built; how strong and fierce we already are.

To move our minds to a better place also involves *trusting our instincts.*

In challenge 3, we're going to explore how leaders with unreasonable ambition can tap into their 'spidey senses'[35] to anticipate their next big move. The blending of intuition and rational decision-making is a key mind tool these leaders actively cultivate to create and maintain strategic competitive edge and keep themselves out of trouble (sometimes!).

It's also what propels them to trust themselves so they can jump into the dark, even in the face of impending uncertainty.

## Reflection

- Being able to successfully adapt to new situations requires a conscious mental shift. For example, if you visit a foreign country where cars drive on the other side of the road, how quickly can you adapt and get behind the wheel without getting into a collision?

- How do you intentionally and consciously switch mental gears when faced with adaptive challenges?

# DON'T BE THERE WHEN THE HURRICANE HITS

I imagine having that sixth sense, the certainty that what I am looking for is within reach, even if it's hidden.

– JODI PICOULT

Just about everyone has heard what happened to Kodak. It's gut-wrenching, and a great example of what can eventuate in the face of big life disruptions when we view the world through a straw.

For almost a century Kodak was at the forefront of photography. It pumped out hundreds of inventions and innovations, making the art of photography accessible to all. As early as 1962, Kodak reached sales of US$1 billion – that's extraordinary, even by today's standards. By 1976 it had become so gargantuan it practically pushed all its competitors out of the market. By 1981, it had reached sales of US$10 billion.

But what was Kodak really selling? It wasn't selling low-cost cameras. Its soaring profits were based on high-volume film sales, and the cultivating of an unhealthy customer dependence on needing to have their photos printed to see them.

Kodak maintained a myopic view of the world, notwithstanding the advent of digital technology in the early 1980s. It continued to print images despite the market's deafening cues, as consumers turned away from paper prints in preference for sharing photos online and at scale.

Kodak's most memorable moment was when it sunk its legacy by failing to recognise what business it was *really* in. The company believed it was in the physical business of printing photos, when it was actually in the emotional business of making memories.

And then, these prophetic words from *The Economist*: 'After 132 years [Kodak] is poised, like an old photo, to fade away.'[36]

## BLINDED BY DISRUPTION

The Kodak story is a sobering example of the stark truth of disruption. Quite simply: if you don't evolve, you will quickly become irrelevant. Business models are changing faster than ever before, and Kodak's demise teaches us that we must keep pace to survive, and disrupt to thrive.

From the outside looking in, the writing on the wall was so clear to those who were watching. Yet Kodak failed to zoom out from its existing world view to see above the clouds.

Have you ever found yourself standing at your pantry looking for the jar of peanut butter you just bought, but you can't find it?

You search the shelves and you just can't see it. You start to get flustered; you know it's there, but where? Finally, in exasperation, you remark, 'Where's that damn peanut butter?' Someone walks over, picks up the jar and hands it to you. The jar was right in front of you all along (and you suddenly feel very foolish!).

What prevented you from seeing that jar of peanut butter?

In that moment, fear took over; fear of not finding the jar. Fear shuts down your ability to see what is right in front of your eyes. In those moments of frenetic scanning, your vision becomes blurry, your decision-making is impaired and your ability to execute is stalled.

Psychologically, that's exactly what happened to Kodak. Kodak was unable to evolve because the fear of change was holding it back from making the necessary shifts it needed to reinvent itself and carve out a new playing field in the memory-making business.

Evolution is personal. Evolution is change. Change is fear. And to overcome it requires you to *get out of your own way.*

---

**Evolution is personal. Evolution is change. Change is fear. And to overcome it requires you to get out of your own way.**

---

This challenge is focused on preparing you for the enormity of what's possible. I want to get you mentally ready to take the plunge and set the course for a future that is largely unknown. If it sounds like a daunting challenge, that's because it is! (I did warn you to be ready for anything in this book!)

## QUIT EQUALS GRIT

My years of field research and observation into the unreasonably ambitious mindset have revealed undisputed evidence of a resounding behaviour pattern. People with unreasonable ambition anticipate the warning signs and get out of the way of a hurricane (literally and figuratively!) before it hits.

They use quitting for competitive advantage.

Now, I acknowledge that we are not all faced with frequent life-threatening situations. So, what might a more relatable example be?

Think about a company that starts laying people off. (Just as a sidebar, I spent years essentially doing the job George Clooney played out in *Up in the Air* – I was hired to be the hatchet woman to support people being laid off. In truth, it was the worst job I have ever had; dirtier even than another job I had, cleaning tables at a Swedish restaurant dressed in a dairy maid costume to pay off my student loans!) It's fascinating to witness how some people in the organisation are smart enough to jump ship and find a new job before they get the axe and things really turn to mud.

But how do these people know when it is time to jump?

What I have come to learn is that these folks have the ability to take in new information so they can make decisions about their future reality with informed eyes, and without blinkers on. They pick up on subtle cues and signals and see a pattern emerging that suggests their days are numbered. Then they act.

Research into the benefits of quitting demonstrates how unreasonably ambitious leaders also have the habit of setting 'kill criteria' before they even start a job, an investment or a relationship.[37] Kill criteria are red flags these leaders identify that are signs that things aren't going to plan and their efforts are outweighing the benefits. It's a sobering realisation that there's limited return on their investment of energy, time and resources. This involves being able to read the signs more clearly, as well as putting a concrete deadline in place for getting out of a situation that's not working for them.

We are going to unpack how to develop this skill next. We'll start by learning how to listen to the future to make decisions about bold strategic plays. Then you'll discover how leaders with unreasonable ambition proactively build their hyperawareness and draw on their sense-making skills to anticipate critical trends in motion to bend the world to their goals.

After that we'll dive into the unfathomable; into a realm that rarely gets a mention in the C-suite. We'll explore how leaders with unreasonable ambition rely heavily on their intuition to proactively plan for and predict the future and take advantage of shifting market tides.

We'll finish up with tips on execution: making informed decisions that will steer you in the right direction at speed. Leaders with unreasonable ambition are always drawing from their peripheral vision to connect the dots going backwards, so they can take giant leaps forward into the dark to execute the impossible.

# CHAPTER 15

# LISTENING TO THE FUTURE

In a time of drastic change, it is the learners who inherit the future. The learned usually find themselves equipped to live in a world that no longer exists.

– ERIC HOFFER

I've been working with leaders for so long I can literally hear the 'song' of someone who listens to the future to plan their next big move. It's as if their brain is wired differently, giving them the ability to see patterns and make connections not obvious to others. It involves a dexterous interweaving of intuition, sensing and empirical data that drives bold decisions that often lead to product, service or industry reinvention.

It's the sweetest sound.

Jeff Melanson is one of Canada's leading arts leaders and serial entrepreneurs, and a creativity and innovation columnist for HuffPost. He's a partner of the Stratagem Group, an Ontario-based film production company that recently launched its first Hollywood blockbuster, *Mayor of Kingston*, with Paramount Pictures.[38] He is a Jury member at the Cannes Film Festival. He's also a strategic partner to Unity, the company leading the world in metaverse technology solutions that would blow your mind. His innovative enterprise saw him build Quaver Music – a virtual music education platform which he then flipped, but not before being heralded as a smaller company with a 'high trust stack' that managed to 'pull off an Uber', creating 'both supply with demand, powering an entirely new, modern business model'.[39]

I have been standing alongside Melanson for over a decade, watching his epic falls and gargantuan leaps forward. He is an impressive individual who has reinvented both himself and the creative industries that have had the privilege of his insights. Melanson is the quintessential phoenix rising up from the ashes – from experiences that set him aflame to be reborn. He even has a bird tattooed on his back: a raven, which is said to foreshadow change.

What I have noticed about unreasonably ambitious leaders like Melanson is the speed at which they can make sense of their external environments. They build an almost premonition-like ability to cast future scenarios with impressive accuracy. Just like the raven permanently inked into his skin, Melanson has sustainably kept up with the pace of change by building his ability to learn faster than the world evolving around him.

But just *how* does he do it?

I know it kind of sounds ethereal, unattainable even. But let me break it down for you so it feels less out of reach.

## THRIVING IN VUCA ENVIRONMENTS

The vast body of research conducted by acclaimed business school IMD clarifies the specific capabilities required to build these soothsayer-like business skills.[40] Empirical data fuelling its publicly available Agile Leader Model found that leaders who demonstrate greater effectiveness through periods of disruption and are more likely to thrive in VUCA environments demonstrate four characteristics: *humility, adaptability, vision* and *engagement*.[41]

The research also identified three key behaviours that help these leaders successfully navigate disruptive environments:

1.  **Hyperawareness:** Constantly scanning internal and external environments for opportunities and threats.
2.  **Making informed decisions:** Making use of data and information to make evidence-based decisions.
3.  **Executing at speed:** Moving quickly, often valuing speed over perfection.

Not surprisingly, it was found that leaders who scored more highly on the key characteristics and behaviours identified tended to significantly outperform other leaders on measures such as work engagement and leadership effectiveness.

What's Melanson's take on this? Melanson is at his core a boffin who is voraciously curious about the world. He is a lover of stories past and present and he does his homework. He says:

> *Study and deeply observe both trajectory and history. Understand how you got here; what factors made you win and lose past chapters. Be aware enough to know that things you did successfully in the past might not work; and likewise, that a past failed experiment may have been too early or not used in the right context.*

Melanson is also a big believer in lifelong learning to build strategic agility: 'Consume copious amounts of information across sectors. Patterns will become evident.'

To be able to make sense of what's going on around him, Melanson is militant in his discipline around carving out time and space to think. 'Stand very still,' he says. 'When you're in motion it is hard to see the moves of the world.' He also speaks to the perils of hubris and bringing ego into leadership: 'Lose the ego. You probably don't know what you are doing.'

What is illuminating about Melanson's story is how he has developed his own powerful philosophy that acts as a guide for unreasonably ambitious leadership in modern times. At a deeper level, his views also express the danger of expert-led leadership approaches, and technical organisations that over-rely on black-and-white problem-solving.

Adopting the mindset of a learner – one that is *ego-less* – is the secret to remaining agile and maintaining edge in life and business. The alternative is to continue to believe that you have all the answers; that you alone can solve the problems of today's complex business environment, that will continue to be unpredictable and uncontrollable. To hold these beliefs means limiting your ability to lead and succeed in a world where you really don't have a bloody clue.

No-one does.

## Reflection

· How often do you carve out space for reflection in your day?

· What action do you take to create moments of stillness in your life to better 'see the moves of the world'?

· Do you typically reply on your existing toolkit to solve for tomorrow's challenges or do you broaden your range and seek extended input?

· How do you demonstrate curiosity?

- Do your people feel comfortable bringing creative – possibly even wacky – ideas to you for your consideration? Or do you feel as if you are leading in a vacuum at times, with minimal contributions from others? Are you a lone voice? If you're a lone voice, what is it about your approach that is shutting others down from sharing their ideas with you?

# CHAPTER 16

# UNLOCKING YOUR SPIDEY SENSES

The intuitive mind is a sacred gift, and the rational mind is a faithful servant. We have created a society that honors the servant and has forgotten the gift.

– ALBERT EINSTEIN

There's a reason some of my clients call me a witch.

I can imagine what you are thinking right now. *A witch? What on earth…?*

A good witch, of course; not some Maleficent-type character swathed in black with razor-sharp teeth and yellow werewolf eyes, but more of the pure healer-type version.

You see, I've always just known things; heard the unspoken; sensed deeper feelings and intent. I can look straight into someone's heart and understand what they want and whether they are to be trusted (that's the spooky part!). It's a blessing and a curse, if I'm honest. There are some days where I have wished I could have been blind to my visions.

As a child, being able to read others' emotions was quite scary at times. I could feel how other people were feeling as if it were me. It was confusing and draining. I would run away and hide, trying to escape from the intensity of what I was sensing. It was overwhelming for a little girl, and the only way I knew how to cope was to steer clear of people.

It wasn't until much later in life that I realised I was a little different to others; that I experienced the world in a more colourful and intense way. After a couple of hospital visits for exhaustion and stomach ulcers in my 20s, I realised that while my insights helped me navigate the sensitivities of relationships, they were also a gift that needed to be managed. Otherwise I ran the risk of getting swallowed up by them.

These days I refer to my gift as intuition. It's a 'spidey sense' that I utilise to work with my clients, helping them to tap into their authentic selves and be better humans. Don't forget, I am a trained scientist-practitioner; but history and experience have taught me the benefits of relying on both data and my instincts in decision-making, rather than becoming a slave to my intellect and the need to be right. Both have served me well.

I was delighted to read that Bill Gates cited his reliance on intuition as enabling him to reach new heights in business success. So, I can't be judged as a complete nut job, right?

## INTUITION IS YOUR MOST UNDERUTILISED RESOURCE

What exactly is intuition, and can it be developed by anyone?

Research has demonstrated that intuition is more than just a gut feeling. It is the ability to tap into both your data-rational and unconscious minds to consider all your options before making a decision. Intuition is finally getting some attention by Oxford scholars, with intuitive intelligence being deemed as 'perhaps the greatest weapon for business decision-making'.[42] It's also a capability that, when nurtured, will yield the most spectacular blossoms of insight.

And there it is. In an age where we require agility and the ability to make sense of and respond to a world on hyper speed, leaders must learn how to tap into an *innate source of wisdom* – one that is not well understood, nor being leveraged fully.

In chapter 15 I shared the concept of hyperawareness with you. If you recall, cultivating hyperawareness is being able to stand still to take in, absorb and see patterns and trends in your external ecosystems. It's all about understanding context. To do this successfully requires you to listen to the movement of information around you, so that you can make predictions about what's coming and interpret the play with greater accuracy.

Unreasonably ambitious leaders tend to embrace rather than discount their intuitive intelligence. They have trust in their insights and know how to channel them to spark greater clarity and strategic foresight.

**Unreasonably ambitious leaders tend to embrace rather than discount their intuitive intelligence.**

Unreasonably ambitious leaders are confident enough in themselves to let their intuition guide them. By listening to their inner voice, they can tap into early warning signals to drive enhanced and more holistic outcomes. They are also more effective people leaders, connecting to the hearts and minds of those they serve.

## Reflection

· How much do you rely on your intuition to make decisions? Do you listen to your intuitive intelligence or discount it?

· Can you recall times when you have ignored your intuition and you wish you hadn't? What would the outcome have been if you'd listened? What decisions would you have made differently and for the better with the benefit of hindsight?

## THE PATH TO INTUITIVE ENLIGHTENMENT

Are you feeling curious?

It's possible to actively develop your intuitive intelligence. In my leadership practice I endorse committing to daily meditation and mindfulness to make way for enhanced intuition. Channelling their ancient wisdom helps my clients lead more holistically with their whole selves.[43]

Keeping a journal and recording insights and visual images as they happen is also a good habit to get into. Neuroscience research suggests that intuitive insights that are not immediately captured may never be recalled again. I keep a journal next to my bed to record the images I might receive during my own mindfulness rituals or in my dreams. Sometimes my visuals happen in the moment as well. There have been many times during my career that I have freaked out clients when I've shared the images that I see in my mind that feel like they come out of left field.

I was once working with a high-paid executive who was very resistant to being coached. In truth, he was not someone I would normally work with (I don't do remedial or 'fixer-upper' coaching), however his boss had begged me to have one session with him in the hope that I would change my mind and take him on.

During the session the client sat with his arms crossed, grunting and snarling at me. His responses to my questions were monosyllabic.

His energy was confrontational and awkward. I couldn't wait to get out of there!

I said to him: 'It feels like we are wasting our time here today. You seem angry and closed to working with me. I would like to propose we call it quits and get on with our day. But before you go, I would like to ask you one last question. I'd like to know what happiness looks like for you.'

Before he could answer, an image flashed up in my mind of a beautiful sailboat on the ocean.

I spoke (without thinking): 'I'm guessing you'd prefer to be sailing on the water today rather than being here talking to me.'

He looked at me in utter disbelief. 'What did you say? How did you know I love to sail?' He was shaking, looking at me with an incredulous gaze as if I was an apparition.

'I didn't,' I said.

There was silence. And then, tears started rolling down his cheeks.

He shared with me that he was miserable. He was working so much that he didn't have time to do the things he was passionate about, or be with the people he loved. When the floodgates opened, his soul cracked open for the light to shine through.

I am not a magician. I am not a witch and I do not have mystical powers. What I do have is an ability to open the door between my subconscious and conscious mind much wider to receive deeper sources of insight that go beyond my logical brain.

Reflecting on how I might have known this man enjoyed sailing, I am not entirely sure. It may have been his tanned skin. Perhaps that he had windswept blonde hair, or that he was gruff like an old sea captain. Regardless, the image that conjured in my mind helped him to get in touch with what was missing most in his life; where he needed to refocus his energy to be happy. And that was all that mattered to me.

In that moment, my intuition was my soul's voice whispering truth to this frustrated sailor, hoping that he would hear.

And he did.

# CHAPTER 17

# JUMPING INTO THE DARK

Sometimes to change a situation you are in requires you to take a giant leap. But you won't be able to fly unless you are willing to transform.

– SUZY KASSEM

Just checking in to see that you are still with me.

I hope you are feeling excited by the adventure I am inviting you to join me on – to quieten the noise, eliminate the unimportant and focus on taking the leadership of your life and work to an elevated level of magic.

Once you have listened to the signals around you and inside your head, linked all the new ideas and come up with a strategy to tackle the future, it's about what you *do* with that information. An idea remains an idea unless you put it into action. And it may be a bad idea; you won't know if you don't test it, and re-test it – if you don't question everything.

And that is one of the defining characteristics of leaders with unreasonable ambition – the persistent and maniacal focus on the execution of ideas that are often viewed as 'outrageous' or 'impossible'. The unreasonably ambitious hold the belief that one of them will land. To bring 'crazy', untested, new ideas into the world takes courage and a high tolerance for risk, as well as a willingness to undergo intense scrutiny – not an experience for the faint of heart!

Realising big ideas is something business owners do all the time. One of my ridiculously talented entrepreneur clients who has launched several multimillion-dollar businesses over several decades says, 'Starting a business is like eating glass and staring into the abyss' – ain't that the truth!

I attended an innovation leadership workshop a couple of years ago facilitated by the super-engaging and wildly charismatic Brit, Andy Lamb. He's the epitome of thinking big and personal reinvention. He went from being an Australian tour promoter for iconic electronic dance band The Prodigy to a professional corporate career for Wall Street financial services companies, and is now one of Australia's leading educators in creativity and innovation. His saying on innovation is gold: 'All ideas are shit, until they're not.' There's power in the simplicity of this statement!

I am sure Lamb would attest to the fact that getting yourself into the right headspace or flow zone to make stuff happen requires steely mental discipline. Much like any other habit you want to build, having acute self-awareness and practising getting into the flow mindset is how you embed this type of thinking into your neural hardwiring. It's a process of becoming, where innovation is just another part of who you are.

Granted, this may sound a little 'out there' – especially to those of you reading who are more left-brained – but I can assure you that a ton of research exists in this area.

## Reflection

·   How many ideas do you come up with before you implement one? For the record, on average only one good idea realises into an awesome opportunity in every 2000 ideas!

·   How do you stay the course once you move to idea execution? What keeps you motivated?

·   How do you test your ideas to make sure they are desired by your target customer and not just something you think is a cool thing to do?

## CONVERTING RADICAL IDEAS TO IMPACTFUL CHANGE

The work of author and flow researcher Steve Kotler resonates with me. He coined a term for this style of mental processing: 'moonshot thinking'.[44] He defines moonshot thinking using the following equation:

*Creativity + Pattern Recognition + Risk = Moonshot Thinking*

His findings have illustrated that it's not enough to just listen to the future and develop clear predictive insights; *it's what you do with them that matters.* It's through execution that you activate powerful neurochemical reactions to tap deeper into your flow zone.

If you want to experience more neural flow in your life you must choose to think differently. It's about being prepared to do the work to connect ideas together and then being courageous enough to launch your big ideas into the world – knowing you will be judged!

Here's a suggestion: instead of tackling problems the way you always have, try doing something completely different and see where you land. Unreasonably ambitious leaders go out of their way to deliberately stretch their imaginations – it's a conscious choice.

---

**Unreasonably ambitious leaders go out of their way to deliberately stretch their imaginations.**

---

## INCREASE YOUR APPETITE FOR RISK-TAKING AND AMBIGUITY

If you really want to increase your courage and tolerance for risk-taking and ambiguity, a fun coaching challenge I set for my clients is to commit to a *year of yes*.

What does this look like exactly? Committing to a year of yes means saying an emphatic yes to every opportunity or experience that is offered to you, no matter what it is, and letting go of control. The personal transformation I have seen in clients taking on this challenge is unbelievable. (My disclaimer here is that you don't agree to do anything illegal or harmful!)

I will never forget when I did this. It just happened to be at the same time as the erotic novel *Fifty Shades of Grey* was released, and I was invited to attend a Fifty Shades 'party'. I had no idea what I was getting myself into. Within a few minutes of entering the house it became clear that it wasn't a book club!

Those who really know me would never describe me as having a vanilla personality, but this experience pushed even a rebel like me way out of my comfort zone. It made me sweat, and it took every ounce of self-restraint to resist the inclination to get the hell out of there!

Instead, I chose a new response. I chose to stay – squirming and wriggling in the discomfort until the very end. I was the last person to leave. I was very proud of myself because it was tough to stay put!

So, why did I choose to stay? Am I just a sucker for punishment?

Psychologically, the experience helped me increase my tolerance for discomfort. When I left I felt invigorated and was surging with adrenaline. It was fantastic!

## CHASING RAINBOWS

To be able to think outrageously big, we humans must massively up the amount of novelty in our lives. Research shows that it's new environments and experiences that are often the jumping-off points for new ideas. Doing new things creates more opportunity for pattern recognition and uncovering of novel, sometimes world-changing, ideas that are yet to be realised.

Now don't get me wrong: actively seeking new experiences and exposure to different operating contexts doesn't have to provide you with the mind-altering experience that I just shared with you. It could be as simple as travelling to a country where you don't speak the language, engaging in an activity where you have to learn something new, or networking with people outside of your industry sector where you have no apparent common interests or things to talk about.

To bring us back to world of work, most business innovations come from disruption and yet the majority of market-leading organisations are unable to make that jump and adapt to the changes going on around them. Organisations need to figure out how they can jump from current opportunities to new opportunities, or risk getting left behind.

Radical change requires radical action. It's as simple as that.

Radical change requires radical action.

## BLOW YOURSELF UP

For leaders, radical action requires a deep commitment to self-innovate. If you are to jump s-curves and capitalise on what lies before you, you must actively boost your readiness for extreme and unorthodox possibilities.

An s-curve of revenue growth is where a business starts out slowly, grows rapidly until it approaches market saturation, before levelling off. The secret of high-performing companies is that they learn how to jump the curve.

Intentionally seeking out opportunities to disrupt yourself and your thinking lays the foundation for staying relevant and fresh. In his book *Range*, David Epstein outlines the perils of the expert mindset which offers only siloed thinking and will fail to flourish in our current world context. In contrast, he says that it is the most impactful inventors who think more broadly and seek out diverse experiences and perspectives to thrive.[45]

So, I encourage you to give yourself permission to jump into the dark more often, knowing that each jump will unlock the creative potential needed to take you to new and even more exciting places.

## Reflection

- How do you intentionally push yourself out of your comfort zone to stretch your thinking?

- How has reaching into your existing toolbox as a default stunted opportunities for growth and expansion?

- Can you think of moments in your life where you have lived bravely? Have any of these experiences been catalysts for major sliding-door experiences that have changed the course of your life?

# CHALLENGE 4

# A LEAP OF FAITH

They can, because they think they can.

– VIRGIL

There is no doubt that life, particularly over the last decade, has rocked humanity to its core. Within the cycle of life and death, it seems as if the world has been cracked wide open. We've had recurring existential challenges, some threatening our very existence. Many of us have struggled to hang on to any shred of optimism; to keep our heads above water and stay the course.

And yet, being able to stick to a resolve of possibility and relentlessly pursue all that that our world still has to offer is often what drives *unreasonably ambitious* leaders. It's this mindset that allows them to rise above the masses to higher ground, while others are smothered in a shroud of darkness – drowning in the negativity of the 'non-believers' who have lost the faith and will to strive.

Non-believers are toxic, their negativity contagious. I have a pet name for these people: Chicken Littles. They are people who expect calamity and disaster without justification. And they're everywhere.

Leaders with what I call Chicken Little Syndrome are tough to work with. Their feelings of helplessness and negativity result in a kind of mental paralysis, blocking not only their own ability to succeed but also the efforts of everyone who has the misfortune to encounter them.

I will admit, as much as I would classify myself more of a Mary Poppins-type character (it is hard to keep me down for long), it remains a perpetual challenge for me to work constructively with Chicken Littles. I find it hard to resist the urge to show them the door and wipe them off my radar.

It is not surprising then that unreasonably ambitious leaders also struggle to engage with the naysayers of this world. The magnanimous Frank Cooper, an Officer of the Order of Australia and West Australian of the Year, once shared with me his term for these types of people – he called them 'dementors'. 'You know, like in Harry Potter?' he said. 'The ones who suck the air out of the room, that you want to run from.'

## SWINGS AND ROUNDABOUTS

There is no doubt that life can be fraught with staggered moments of jubilation and sheer terror; but it is *a lack of belief in our own ability to succeed* that is one of the biggest blockers hindering our ability to evolve. It's like the story of Peter Pan: when people stopped believing in him, his magic disappeared and he was forgotten.

I once had a conversation about this with former Walt Disney Corporation executive and adjunct professor at UC Berkeley Pat Reed. She was the executive coach and transformation lead supporting Walmart in their mammoth turnaround several years back.

You may have heard about it: the battle between Walmart and Amazon, two retail giants competing for the number-one spot.[46] It all came about when Amazon decided to diversify its assets, moving away from a total technology business to acquiring the grocery chain Whole Foods Market to try to outrun Walmart. Since then, Walmart has kept its dominant position by a nose; but what it has had to overcome to get there is the more interesting story.

It may surprise you to learn that the biggest challenge Walmart faced in its battle against Amazon *was not financial.* Neither was it about competence, or quality of product and services.

It was the *battle raging within.*

The core and pervasive belief was that the retail giant was too big to evolve, and that there were too many people, systems and processes to shift to make sustainable progress possible. At a deeper level, one could say that Walmart lacked faith in its inherent ability to outsmart Amazon and build the speed and agility it needed to stay in the retail game.

And yet, it got there. Reed told me that the company's future-focused pivot was due in large part to being willing to question everything around their existing ways of working, thinking and leading. It knew that it would have to blow up everything that failed to create value and put energy only into what mattered most – to become a light-touch, customer-driven and people-first business dedicated to exceptional customer experiences and satisfaction.

Walmart's story is a sobering reminder of the fact that size and dominance don't guarantee longevity in business. If it did, dinosaurs would still be roaming the earth, right? Its success also reinforces the power of self-belief to accomplish exceptional results – or, as Reed puts it, 'achieving the impossible'.

But it demanded a *radical shift in perspective*.

Courtesy of Martin Barnes – Start-Up Pitches

In challenge 4 we will be exploring techniques to build strong self-belief and faith in your ability to succeed in a world dominated by non-believers (which may sometimes be you) who have lost their way. We will unpack the psychology of how being 'delusional' and 'a little bit crazy' correlates to engaging in riskier pursuits and achieving unbelievable performance outcomes.

We will delve further into the concept of self-worth and how unreasonably ambitious leaders take charge to become the directors of this show called life, versus the actors on the stage.

We'll talk about how a mindset of growth and possibility allows us to build *transilience* – the ability to shift from one mental state to another; to be able to think differently, big and beyond.

# CHAPTER 18

# BE DELUSIONAL

'Have I gone mad?'

'I'm afraid so. But I'll tell you a secret. All the best people are.'

– *ALICE IN WONDERLAND* (2010 FILM)

Famous coach and author Marshall Goldsmith did a study of extremely successful people. He found they have one thing in common: they are all slightly delusional.[47] During one of his seminars, he spoke with me about how his research demonstrated that those who thrive on the edge of the unknown have very strong self-belief. He describes them as being in a perpetual state of self-delusion, where even if they don't have all the answers, they will find a way to figure it out no matter how seemingly impossible.

The ability to deal with and navigate ambiguity has been emphatically declared by many top CEOs and entrepreneurs globally as the single-biggest predictor of executive success. What's interesting about Goldsmith's work is the double-edged sword that is also inherent in tales of executive success. That while the great confidence that arises from success propels leaders to trust themselves more and take riskier moves, it can also prevent them from evolving – making them a *victim of their own success*.

We will explore how ego can get in your way in subsequent chapters. For now, I would like to go back to that word *delusional*.

When you read the word 'delusional', do you have an immediate association with idea of *madness*? Your brain may have naturally wandered towards thoughts of the mentally ill or deranged – and you would not be wrong in going there. I mean, let's face it, there is irrefutable evidence to support the fact that many of the world's most celebrated minds, artists and creatives have suffered from some type of neurological challenge or undiagnosed chronic mental illness. Being super brainy or a creative thinker has seen many of the greats excommunicated, socially ostracised or burnt at the stake over the centuries.

One only has to think of John Nash, the Nobel Prize-winning mathematician who suffered from schizophrenia; or artist Vincent Van Gogh, who sliced off his ear during a supposed psychotic episode; or tortured soul Frida Kahlo, who was thought to suffer from an array of mental illnesses causing her to develop a 'peculiar, disruptive and intense personality' (labels that could also mean she was an imaginative, passionate nonconformist!).

These extraordinary leaders represent traditional notions of what it typically means to be delusional – and the perils of not sharing your creative gifts with the world so they're only discovered after you're dead!

## THERE'S METHOD IN MADNESS

People who think differently have not, until very recently, been celebrated. The Fourth Industrial Revolution brought with it greater acknowledgement that creativity and outlier thinking are capabilities to be coveted.

Scientific evidence provides strong support for the linear correlation between IQ (or 'genius') and mental illness. What this means is that the more of a brainiac you are, the more likely you are to be at risk of affective 'hyper brain' psychological disorders such as attention deficit hyperactivity disorder (ADHD), autism spectrum disorder (ASD) or bipolar.[48]

We need more unreasonably ambitious leaders to challenge outmoded ways of thinking and unlock creative potential if we are to open more doorways to possibility. In today's ill-defined world, with no clear guidelines and armed only with an internal compass, leaders have an enormous leap to take. They must rely more heavily on their instincts and have the courage to venture into uncharted terrain, knowing that failure is inevitable.

This could very well be considered an act of madness, could it not? Why would you catapult yourself into new frontiers knowing that at first you are more likely to fail than succeed, or maybe even get excommunicated by your peers.

And yet, if you cast your mind back to challenge 1: embracing the suck, to think like an unreasonably ambitious leader is to simultaneously embrace reality and be driven by an overriding belief that anything is possible – irrespective of evidence that may point to the contrary. That's the distinction between leaders who choose reasonableness and mediocrity over following their unreasonable ambitions. Leaders with unreasonable ambition will champion originality and take action to propel the world forward, without hesitation. Their desire to advance is stronger than their doubts. It outweighs their fears and compels them to reach for more.

---

**Unreasonably ambitious leaders' desire to advance is stronger than their doubts. It outweighs their fears and compels them to reach for more.**

---

Unreasonably ambitious leaders have learned to overcome the emotions that prevent us humans from trying to realise something that goes against the grain. It is not that they don't see the potential pitfalls, dangers or improbability; they are, in fact, completely in touch with reality. It's that they fundamentally trust themselves to find a solution and figure it out. *They are willing to give just about anything a red-hot go.*

Part of the skill of generating new insights lies in the willingness to seek out broader perspectives and ask for help. It's knowing that while their individual insights may be sound, tapping into vast and collective intelligence will catapult their thinking to the next level.

This is probably one of the biggest blockers for leaders trained in more technical ways of thinking and doing. Jostein Solheim, CEO Health and Wellbeing at Unilever, said: 'For people who like the linear route forward, life is getting harder and harder, in any field.'[49] The gravitational pull of the need to know can seriously thwart these leaders' ability to dance in the grey.

## SILVER SPOONS AND SMARTS DON'T GUARANTEE ADVANTAGE

In his book *Originals: How Non-Conformists Change the World*, Adam Grant shares some research on child prodigies. These children are never the ones who end up changing the world, because while they are 'often rich in both talent and ambition' they have never learned to be original in their thinking.[50] To paraphrase TS Eliot, their careers tend to end 'not with bang but a whimper'.[51]

What is clear to me, having worked with dazzling changemakers over a couple of decades, is that most of them were not unusually gifted children; nor did they do things by the book. They were unlikely to have been favoured by their teachers and, in many cases, were considered the troublemakers or proverbial crap bags. They often made up their own rules and chose a risky pursuit of the novel, without any obvious support.

Michael Dell of Dell Computers is a well-known example of this type of youngster. When he told his father he wanted to start a computing business and drop out of university, his dad thought he was mad. But Dell had a vision to become the world's leading manufacturer of computer software – and he did. At 27 years of age, he was ranked as the top CEO in business by many of the world's leading publications. He is now estimated to be worth close to US$60 billion.

Dell's story is not unusual. I have worked with countless unreasonably ambitious leaders who were deemed by society as school dropouts; who didn't enjoy institutionalised learning and never quite fitted in. I have also worked with people of average to high intelligence who have equally made their mark on this world.

What is powerful is that all these leaders were *grossly underestimated* at some point in their lives. They are the unexpected success stories who challenge our biases about the prerequisites we ascribe to 'successful' people. They remind us that we are all capable of greatness – if we believe enough in ourselves, leave our egos at the door and are relentless in chasing new opportunities.

The truth is that success is a highly romanticised notion. And for every success story there are hundreds, even thousands, more failures. Think of James Dyson, who produced more than 5000 rejected prototypes; Walt Disney, who was told he lacked imagination; or JK Rowling, a single mother on welfare with zero writing credits who is now worth an estimated US$1 billion.

**Success is a highly romanticised notion.**

Coming up next in chapter 19, we'll explore how leaders with unreasonable ambition mentally sustain themselves on their pathway to success by blocking out the noise of inevitable defeat and focusing instead on achieving unparalleled success.

## Reflection

· What kind of a student were you in school? Did you respond well to traditional teaching methods or feel bored, your mind wandering? Understanding how you learn is a critical contributor to being successful.

· If school or higher education wasn't for you, how does not getting that piece of paper play into your self-confidence as an adult? Does it hold you back from going after opportunities?

· Have you had moments in your life where you've felt like you're the only one who 'gets it'? How have you backed yourself in those moments? How did you convince others of your beliefs to get support around execution?

· If you don't get it right the first time, how do you respond? Do you give up altogether or does it energise you to try again or test a different approach?

# CHAPTER 19

# LIFE IS A STAGE

Art, especially the stage, is an area where it is impossible to walk without stumbling. There are in store for you many unsuccessful days and whole unsuccessful seasons: there will be great misunderstandings and deep disappointments... you must be prepared for all this, expect it and nevertheless, stubbornly, fanatically follow your own way.

– ANTON CHEKHOV

Don't believe everything you read.

There is a psychological price to being an unreasonably ambitious leader. Life can be brutal, and yet many successful leaders and entrepreneurs – the likes of Elon Musk and Mark Zuckerberg – still achieve hero status today. While we may idolise these types of leaders, the truth is that many harbour secret demons, near-debilitating anxiety and despair they don't admit to.

In our culture we've learned that to share vulnerability is taboo. Instead, leaders are socialised to 'fake it until they make it', hoping – no, praying – that good fortune will smile upon them. They rely on their sophisticated skills of impression management to see them through – until they *do* make it. But it takes a huge emotional toll, and not one that is easy to bounce back from.

Let's take entrepreneurs as an example. Being an entrepreneur is a highly stressful vocation, and a high risk of failure comes with the job. According to research by Shikar Gosh at Harvard Business School, three out of four venture-backed startups fail, while 95 per cent of startups fall short of initial projections.[52]

What about CEOs of large corporations? With the world reshuffling its priorities and workers leaving organisations in droves, CEOs are under more pressure than ever to think differently about how to scale, succeed and thrive in the coming decade.

There is no doubt that the most successful leaders, the unreasonably ambitious, can quell their fears and silence their inner demons to reach glorious heights – even during an age of intense disruption. But what we might miss is that success does not come without countless false starts, rough landings and an ongoing battle with the duck of doubt; the one that sits quacking on their shoulders, telling them that they are good, but *maybe not good enough*.

## THAT DAMN DUCK OF SELF-DOUBT

Whenever we are dancing in uncertainty and ambiguity, self-doubt always shows up. It's just part of being human. No matter how successful we become, most of us will still have our self-worth tested at some point in our careers (unless we're delusional, in the deranged kind of way!).

Look at it this way. If a stranger came up to you on the street and told you that you were stupid and would probably never succeed at anything in your life, you would probably have no trouble telling them they were wrong. However, when you fail at something and tell *yourself* that you are useless, you believe it to be true.

In the workplace, impostor syndrome is one face of self-doubt that strikes frequently. It's one of the most common coaching issues that presents in my leadership practice, especially in leaders who are unreasonably ambitious.

But what is it exactly and why is it showing up to haunt us?

Impostor syndrome (also known as impostor phenomenon, fraud syndrome or the impostor experience) is when you suffer from an inability to internalise your accomplishments and have a persistent fear of being exposed as a 'fraud'. The phenomenon was first labelled back in 1978 in an academic study that was strictly centred on women who were finally able to put a few cracks in the glass ceiling of male-dominated business leadership. Many of those female executives believed they were only promoted because they were lucky, or judged to be better than they were. The reality was, deep down, they believed they were frauds who would be exposed.[53]

Many people who are catapulted into high-profile positions of power or fame find themselves plagued by feelings of inadequacy and self-doubt. They're just waiting for that tap on the shoulder; for some-one to say, 'Okay, I have figured it out. You're not worthy. Move on!'

I once coached the CEO of a notable global technology organisa-tion in Silicon Valley. He shared with me that he couldn't understand how someone as 'dumb' as him could have fumbled his way into the top job! Yet here he was, changing the very face of the industry as we knew it, and loved by his people.

At the heart of impostor syndrome lies the issue of self-worth and how we measure our own success. Many leaders become trapped in what Insead Professor of Strategy and Innovation Nathan Furness describes as a 'Machiavellian obsession' to be the best and do whatever it takes to achieve goals of money, status and power. With such a single-minded focus on seeking career satisfaction from external reinforcers, these leaders get caught up in a loop of perpetual dissatisfaction. Their self-worth is reliant on outcomes that are constantly shifting and out of reach; *it does not come from within.*

I often ask my clients to describe their perceived value, and explain to me why they believe they get to do the job they do, and have the power and influence they have. I've heard some very interesting responses. But here is the takeaway: the way we speak to ourselves, our internal dialogue, has a significant effect on our confidence in the short term and our self-esteem in the long term.

---

**Our internal dialogue has a significant effect on our confidence and self-esteem.**

---

## SHUT THE DUCK UP!

It is important to realise that your beliefs are just beliefs; not facts. If you can recognise your self-limiting beliefs and negative self-talk you can logically and rationally argue with them to create change. That's what I focus on with my clients who are plagued by impostor syndrome – changing how they speak to themselves, building their inner strength and shifting their locus of control from external to internal.

My own self-worth story involves a major developmental milestone that changed everything for me – my emotional health, the quality of my relationships and the level of courage I had to stand up and take more risks in my life. It's the story of a ball gown, a hobo and a wise Greek grandmother, Yaya (that's the Greek word for grandmother).

At primary school I was the stereotypical happy, fat kid. Coming from a culture where we lived to eat didn't help. While the Australian kids were enjoying their Vegemite sandwiches for lunch, it was not uncommon for me to tuck into an enormous antipasto platter and crusty Italian loaf still fresh from the local bakery. My lunches were delicious, but my eating habits weren't great! I had a nice gaggle of friends and was naturally a jovial person, but on the inside my self-esteem and confidence were fast declining.

Many years later it was the night of my Year 11 ball. I decided to walk a few kilometres down the road to show Yaya how I looked in my ball gown. It was one of the few times during those awkward teenage years that I felt pretty. I had my hair and makeup done and felt like the ugly duckling who had been transformed into a beautiful swan for the night.

On the way to Yaya's house, I passed a very scruffy-looking man sitting at a bus stop. He was making rude comments to people as they walked past. I tried to hurry past unscathed but didn't make it without hearing him snickering. He said, 'Where do you think you're going missy? No-one is going to dance with you in that dress. You look ugly!'

I was shattered. His words hit my heart in successive blows like arrows fired from a bow. My self-esteem under siege, I started to sob, running away from him with tears streaming down my face.

There was no way I was going to the ball looking ugly!

As I arrived at my destination, the door flung open and a perfectly coiffed lady with a radiant smile leaned in to greet me with arms out-stretched. I jumped into her arms. Her face looked confused. Why was her granddaughter standing in her doorway with a tear-soaked face and black mascara running from her eyes?

'Darling, why are you crying?' she asked in a thick Greek accent.

'The man, at the bus stop,' I sobbed, 'He told me I was ugly.'

'Who was this man who told you that you look ugly?'

'I don't know,' I replied. 'Some dirty-looking man. I don't know him.'

She looked at me with a knowing smile and said, 'Some man you don't know? Darling, what are you thinking? Why on earth would you listen to the words of a man with dirty feet?'

It was a lightbulb moment. In that singular instant my perspective was radically altered forever. I recognised how quickly I had handed over my power to someone I didn't even know – without question. My self-esteem was in danger of being in tatters in an instant, all because of a stranger.

These days, I see this often – in leaders, colleagues, friends and family. How often do we look to others for validation and permission? We look to those we have never met to dictate the standards of our lives. We let them tell us how we should act, think and be.

**We look to those we have never met to dictate the standards of our lives.**

That simple comment from a man with dirty feet had melted me into a puddle of insecurity. But here's the gold: his comment wouldn't have taken hold if I hadn't already believed it to be true! Insecurities, self-doubt and shaky self-worth can only take hold if we give them airtime.

So how do you turn your self-talk around? How can you empower yourself with a more emboldened internal narrative?

## LEARNING TO ARGUE WITH YOURSELF

Psychologically speaking, when adversity occurs, our belief about it and how we make sense of it tests the durability of our self-worth. The lens that we choose to view it through makes all the difference in determining whether it will be a positive or negative experience.

When the bus stop man called out to me, I chose to believe that he was right and I was ugly. I had made up my mind not go to my Year 11 ball because of a stranger's negative comments about me. It wasn't until Yaya stepped in that I was able to reframe the situation, realise his words were insignificant and go and enjoy myself with my friends.

Here's another example: if a friend doesn't return your phone call, do you decide it's because they are a bad friend or they don't like you any more, and stew on it and feel bad all day? Or do you decide they haven't called you back because they are really busy, and move on with your day feeling fine and not giving it a second thought?

When we have negative beliefs and they cause negative conse-quences, we have to find a way to dispute the negative beliefs ourselves because, let's face it, most of the time it's only us in the room with no Greek grandmother in sight!

Once I had successfully disputed the negative beliefs I had about the bus stop man's comments, I shifted my mindset, felt more energised and went to the ball committed to having a great time. Consciously shifting my perspective prevented me from becoming the victim – someone that something has happened to. It put me in the driver's seat of my experience, because I ended up choosing my response to it.

In psychology, there is a suite of tools we use to shift mindsets around Chicken Little language. We call these tools disputation techniques. The purpose is to use them to chase away negative thoughts and build a more optimistic and buoyant attitude to life challenges and any experiences that can rattle our self-worth. Here are some questions you can use to shift your mindset:

- **Evidence:** Ask yourself, is there any evidence showing your belief to be true? Is there any evidence showing it to be untrue? For example, before deciding that you are stupid after receiving disappointing feedback on your performance from a manager or direct report, consider the bigger picture of your performance story and other feedback you have received over time.

- **Alternatives:** Most events result from many contributing factors. Chicken Littles tend to latch on to the most permanent, pervasive and personal factors. Looking for other possible alternatives may change your thought patterns. For example, after receiving negative feedback, Chicken Littles may believe that they are bad at their job, while alternatives such as a personality conflict with their boss or direct report or a miscommunication are equally plausible.

- **Implications:** Sometimes things do go wrong through our own fault or failings. It's important to understand the implications of what went wrong. For example, getting negative feedback is unlikely to have drastic negative effects. In times when you can't find appropriate evidence or alternatives to dispute your negative beliefs, take some time and distance to realistically evaluate the implications of the belief.

- **Usefulness:** Being able to recognise when we are holding disruptive beliefs that are simply useless is equally important. It's not always going to be helpful to dwell on beliefs that are not serving you. For example, someone diffusing a bomb may hold the belief that it may go off and they will be killed. Clearly, stewing on that belief may instead hinder their ability to get on with it and should be viewed as unhelpful. This helps the person redirect thoughts in a more positive channel and dismiss the negative thoughts hindering forward momentum.

Being an unreasonably ambitious leader doesn't mean you won't experience moments of doubt. Some may even have you on your knees – you're human, after all. Your emancipation comes from recognising the force of an altered perspective to break the limits of your own beliefs about what you are capable of.

---

**Your emancipation comes from recognising the force of an altered perspective to break the limits of your own beliefs about what you are capable of.**

---

I have a fundamental belief that everyone has some form of hero inside them, and that igniting your inner greatness when the world goes dark is a conscious and life-changing choice. Tennis player Serena Williams was interviewed by journalists about how she gets through moments of shaky confidence. She said, 'You have to believe in yourself when no-one else does.'[54]

In the next chapter we'll get stuck into the nitty-gritty of the power of a growth mindset and how to train your brain to think with unreasonable ambition against the odds.

# Reflection

· If you are looking to prove that the negative thoughts you have about yourself are true you will find validation everywhere. Think about the moments when you have unconsciously handed your power over to the critics in the cheap seats.

· Do you naturally assume that someone in a position of power deserves to be there, or do you wait for them to earn your respect? If you hand over your power to authority figures without question, ask yourself why.

· What are the triggers that cause your duck to quack loudly on your shoulder? What's the source of your self-doubt? What's your evidence for feeling this way?

# CHAPTER 20

# BELIEVING IN MAGIC AND MIRACLES

If I were to wish for anything, I should not wish for wealth and power but for the passionate sense of the potential, for the eye which, ever young and ardent, sees the possible.

– SØREN KIERKEGAARD

Have you heard about the famous Mexican jumping bean experiment? A group of researchers in the US ran an experiment with some Mexican jumping beans. You know what makes the beans jump, right? Inside the beans live the larvae of a small grey moth that has burrowed inside the seed pod and eaten the seed. Once the seed is gone, this larvae has a peculiar fondness for leaping about inside the empty pod, making their new home jump and roll from place to place.[55]

The researchers grabbed a handful of beans, put them in a glass jar and closed the lid. The beans repeatedly jumped to the lid and landed back down again. Researchers were curious to see how high the beans would jump when they took the lid off. The beans catapulted themselves into another series of jumps, never jumping higher than where the lid had once been.

The moral of the story is clear. There are many barriers in life that can prevent us from reaching our potential, real or imagined. In the case of the Mexican jumping beans, they had become conditioned to jump only to the level of the lid. Even when the opportunity arose to jump higher, they stayed within the limits they had learned.

This is a recurring theme for many of us in life: choosing to stay within the comfort of what we know even when previous restrictions have been removed. Choosing to ignore that deep nagging within our souls that urges us to make a change.

But what if we took heed of that inner voice?

What if we listened to that gentle whisper telling us that we all have the capacity to do something extraordinary in life, and then we acted on it? What if we believed we are all capable of so much more?

## DO THE HEAVY LIFTING AND GROW YOUR MINDSET MUSCLE

Earlier in the book we talked about Satya Nadella's monumental turnaround of Microsoft. His secret weapon in the transformation was to focus his leaders on actively developing what's known as a *growth mindset*. This gave them the courage and psychological flexibility to navigate the prevailing winds of change, until they found themselves in calmer waters again.

Nadella's introduction to growth-mindset principles and practices was totally serendipitous, as many magical events are. He is said to have randomly bumped into Carol Dweck, a Stanford Professor of Psychology and expert in motivation and success mindsets, in the corridors of Microsoft one day.

But what is a growth mindset, and how do you know you've got one?

A growth mindset is a state of mind fuelled by the principle that every human being has more energy, talent and potential to deliver. It's a belief that intelligence is not something you have or don't have, but something you can continue to develop. On the flip side is a fixed mindset. It's characterised by a prevailing lack of belief in your own potential to learn, typically resulting in a stunted (or even eliminated) capacity for change and growth.

**A growth mindset is a state of mind fuelled by the principle that every human being has more energy, talent and potential to deliver.**

It is natural for human beings to alternate between both growth and fixed mindsets in their responses to adversity, stress, uncertainty and the unknown. No-one has a growth mindset in every situation, all the time. We're generally a mix of both. It all depends on the situation and how we are triggered by it.

## YOU HAVE A CHOICE

It is *our response* to situations that will lead to lesser or greater success and life fulfilment. And we have a choice in how we respond. For example, a growth-oriented leader is likely to be energised by extreme challenges (progress) while a leader with a fixed mindset is more likely to plateau, give up and lose motivation (regress).

Here's a pedestrian example of this in action. Consider two employees, Bob and Alex, in an annual performance review process that goes bad. Both want to do well, be recognised for a job well done and are likely to be motivated by success and having an impact.

Bob hears the feedback and has a negative reaction to it. His response to the situation is to give up. He retreats from the workplace, taking more sick days, and reduces his efforts to do a good job. Bob sees his efforts as pointless. His ability to evolve and explore alternate approaches to work has been blocked by his belief that his efforts don't make a difference, and that there is nothing he can learn to improve on what he is already doing.

Conversely, Alex is energised by the challenge the feedback presents to do better. She decides to take the feedback on board and puts in extra effort to improve. She is persistent and determined in attaining the enriched goals she has set for herself, and inspired to give her best. Her ability to learn and be innovative has been unlocked by her mindset of growth and possibility.

You can see where this is going. Two employees. Same feedback. Completely different responses.

There is a distinct difference between those who see problems as challenges (see the left column of the following table) and those who see problems as threats and duck for cover (the right column).

## WHEN OUR BRAIN SEES DAILY PROBLEMS...

| Change as a challenge *bring it on!* | Change as a threat *duck for cover!* |
|---|---|
| ▲ Focus on solutions | ▼ Focus on problems |
| ▲ Eyes on outcomes | ▼ Get bogged down in details |
| ▲ Making things better | ▼ Fight to maintain status quo |
| ▲ Open and determined | ▼ Anxious and defensive |
| ▲ Negative emotions energise you | ▼ Negative emotions drain you |
| ▲ Greater engagement | ▼ Disengaged |
| ▲ Hyper productive, accelerated learning | ▼ Learning is blocked |

The world is full of infinite possibilities, but the reality is that *we are all wired to fear big changes*. No-one deals with adversity or uncertainty well. To deal with the shocks of life we have to learn to see the world through fresh eyes, and refocus our play as 'architects of the future, not at the mercy of it.'[56] We must remember that with big change also comes creation, innovation and transformation.

As Dweck explains, 'Having a growth mindset is not a declaration, it's a journey – one that involves small, progressive shifts in thinking, rather than huge leaps.'[57]

## WHAT TRIGGERS YOU?

To kickstart your growth-mindset journey it's important to reflect on the triggers that make you fearful or defensive – that's the sign that your fixed mindset is kicking in, and it's time to get into growth mode. There's no doubt about it, this is tough work. Our work environments can send us mixed messages about how we 'should' show up, and don't always provide the most fertile soil for thinking differently.

When you shift from a fixed to a growth mindset you will experience greater comfort with taking risks and striving for stretch goals. Your stress will reduce, and working relationships will improve – all of which will ultimately lead to enhanced performance.

To build a more consistent growth mindset I have an adaptive challenge for you to try. The focus is on helping you shift your own mindset from fixed to growth. Here are the steps:

1. Catch yourself and pause when you notice your own negative self-talk around a particular scenario or task. For example, you might hear yourself saying things such as 'I can't do this', 'This is too hard' or 'They'll never agree'.

2. Identify where you are on the growth-mindset continuum (https://mindfulbydesign.com/fixed-vs-growth-mindsets). Is there a fixed view that may be holding you back in this situation?

3. Consciously reframe your self-talk through self-reflection, or ask a trusted colleague to chat it through.

4. Observe your own *from-to* shifts. Reflect on the impact the positive self-talk has on your behaviour and the outcome of the situation.

5. Practise this reframing whenever you catch yourself in the fixed-mindset space.

## Reflection

- What did you learn or find out about yourself during this exercise?

- What are you going to do as a result of this exercise?

- Did the exercise help you to feel greater comfort about taking risks and striving for stretch goals?

## SWEATING IT OUT TO GET RESULTS

After doing this exercise you might be feeling like you've done a killer workout. Doing this work can unearth a whole lot of 'stuff' you may have buried over the years that you weren't ready to deal with.

But, if you've done the exercise I designed for you, perhaps even more than once, it is highly probable you have now built up more mind muscle. You'll be a few steps closer to feeling mentally fit and future-ready.

Don't beat yourself up if you don't quite nail the exercise the first time, or even after multiple attempts. The secret is to keep working on it. Everyone is different in terms of their capacity to handle the ebbs and flows of life; but a significant part of mental agility can be learned.[58] My goal is to support you to build a robust mindset that moves you from resilience to a state of *transilience* – where you are able to 'leap from the darkness of the unknown to the brilliance of change, growth and infinite possibility'.[59]

Okay. I'm hoping that you are feeling enlightened and stronger right now. You've just loaded more ammunition into your mental arsenal to ensure you can continue to evolve a future-enabling mindset. You'll be better able to prepare for whatever the future throws at you *before* it happens.

I think you are ready to level up to the next phase of our journey together. So, get comfortable and strap yourself in. You may even wonder why no-one has told you about this before.

# CHALLENGE 5

# SEEING THE FUTURE

Never let the future disturb you. You will meet it, if you have to, with the same weapons of reason which today arm you against the present.

– MARCUS AURELIUS ANTONINUS

If you were to hike through the Rocky Mountain plains at an altitude of 8000 feet you would be forgiven for thinking the landscape was barren, desolate and uninhabited – especially after a long, bleak winter.

This could not be further from the truth.

The decision to persevere with your trek would instead reveal a spectacular sight: arctic flowers adorning the mountainside in the most vivid hues, and all different shapes and sizes. Dwarf alpine columbines are breathtaking flowers that bloom only in high-altitude terrains. These extraordinary mountain plants battle harsh living conditions – high winds, extreme cold, minimal oxygen and intense UV radiation.

The survival of these flowers epitomises the spirit of resilience and agility inherent in nature. The blooms remind us of nature's tenacity to thrive, even while enduring the relentless onslaught of an unpredictable alpine ecosystem.

Human beings are not unlike these alpine flowers. Right now, there is an acute focus on our living in an era of radical change; a time of great unknowns that is forcing us to reboot our mindsets to thrive. We are all standing on the edge of humanity's most extreme challenge. We are being forced to rethink our approach to life and work, and find creative ways to amplify our ability to evolve. Being able to adapt to an unchartered future that involves both people and planet is mission critical if we are to remain on this earth.

We have moved into a period where dynamic new thinking and leading from a more positive and emboldened stance is fundamental to our success. The planet has sent us a stern reminder of what matters most, and is demanding that we evolve into the best versions of ourselves.

**We have moved into a period where dynamic new thinking and leading from a more positive and emboldened stance is fundamental to our success.**

It's asking that we move *beyond resilience* and build our mental agility to move through time, space and place with acute ambidexterity, leveraging our novel experiences to trigger creative adaptation. We must unlock the powers of foresight to be one step ahead of what's coming.

In challenge 5: seeing the future we are going to explore how to amplify our own resilience – even move beyond it – to be better prepared to handle just about anything, no matter how unexpected or unforeseen.

This is a career and life skillset that takes the unreasonably ambitious to an even higher level of psychological functioning and success, even in the face of the most terrifying of situations.

Jump on the high-speed train and hang on for the ride. A more courageous you is about to break through.

# CHAPTER 21

# BUILDING YOUR PRESILIENCE

There is no terror in the bang, only in the anticipation of it.

– ALFRED HITCHCOCK

If the last few years have taught us anything it's how complacent we have become. Dealing with a barrage of black swan events in quick succession emphasised the importance of being able to lead both ourselves and others through unstable conditions.

These ever-morphing times have also reminded us that the way we view resilience is too narrow and limited. The focus has been on becoming resilient to better *endure* negative experiences, rather than flourishing because of them (don't get me started on the mental health system!). A more enlightened state of mind can better inform future-oriented decisions and help shape the post-crisis landscape.

Well-known author Nassim Nicholas Taleb's expanded view of resilience has polarised many, but totally resonates with me. He calls it 'antifragility – the ability not only to recover from shocks but also to grow and flourish from setbacks'. Taleb explains: 'Antifragile is beyond resilience or robustness. The resilient resist shocks and stay the same; the antifragile gains from disorder and gets better.'[60]

## WE ARE SETTING OURSELVES UP TO FALL

Research demonstrating that leaders tend to lose interest in building resilience in their organisations as crises fade concerns me.[61] I worry we will lose all we gained in the show of human strength and advancement during recent times if we fail to solidify lessons learned – and bake resilience, as a minimum, into our DNA.

The garden variety definition of resilience is the ability to endure, withstand or bounce back. From a psychological perspective it boils down to your ability to control your emotions in negative situations. When you experience negative emotions, it heats up your brain, causing it to spark and short-circuit.

So, if we take fear as an example, what typically happens to us when we feel afraid? We shut down. Many of us become immobilised, like statues frozen in motion.

How do you think this affects our ability to learn? To tap into lateral thinking and creativity? Our willingness to take even small risks?

In risky or unknown situations our ability to make sense of what's going on, make good decisions and execute quickly is instantly impaired – *unless* we can quickly self-regulate, cool down these hot emotions and reinterpret what's happening to us in a more positive way.

And that's the mark of an unreasonably ambitious leader, particularly during trying times – to be able to make the shift early, move towards a positive state quickly and work to drive opportunities even in the eye of the storm.

## MOVING BEYOND RESILIENCE

The best way to think of resilience is as a coping response *after* a negative event has happened. I call it 'what we do after we cry'. However, did you know that the more important moment comes *before* the negative event happens? And it's called *presilience.*

Presilience is defined by Dr Gav Schneider as 'an optimal state of knowing, seeing and being which enables us to thrive and evolve in times of seismic paradigm change'.[62] It's an optimised emotional response that prepares us to see what's on the horizon and pragmatically plan for it. I see it as creating a mental springboard to support enhanced strategic foresight, allowing us to practise predictive planning with our ideal future top of mind.

What's fascinating is that much of the work into presilience has been fuelled by years of research looking into the psyche of survivors. Good survivors always concentrate on the present but plan for the future. They expect the best, but they plan for the worst.

Presilient mind control techniques have actually been around for centuries. Accounts of its use to achieve strategic advantage particularly in battle is well-documented – think Samurai warriors, astronauts preparing for a mission to Mars and the US Navy SEALs.

As I am describing this you may start seeing the links between building presilience as a higher-order skill, and growth mindset as the mental state that fuels it – and you would be correct. Having a growth mindset enables you to build presilience skills and is indeed a prerequisite to its successful application.

## HOW IS THE PRESILIENT MIND DIFFERENT?

Presilient people have learned the ability to start controlling their brains before a stressful event happens. They have effectively trained their brains to move into autopilot to deal with stressful situations more optimally. Their brains act like smart thermostats – even before the emotional heat arrives, they provide a burst of cool, calm control that prepares them for the best response.

In other words, the presilient brain is already in calm-down mode before the stress hits. I mentioned bomb experts earlier, and how their minds are calm during the act of diffusing bombs. They achieve this by disrupting their neural hardwiring to respond better to situations that would normally cause them panic.

**The presilient brain is already in calm-down mode before the stress hits.**

Presilience is an active state focused entirely on quick recovery. It's a preventative response we can learn that acts as an alarm bell to let us know that danger might come, and we need to get ready. In contrast, resilience is a more passive response, focused on having grit and with-standing what happens. It's waiting like a sitting duck for the axe to fall. (I know which of these I'd rather cultivate!)

Let me give you an example of presilience in action.

Kevin Brown, former CEO of Perth Airport, had one of the toughest gigs of all: to successfully steer the airport through the Covid-19 crisis with grace, stealth and minimal fallout. With the airport a major centre of employment in Western Australia (with approximately 12,570 aviation-related and 5230 non-aviation-related full-time employees), Brown had his work cut out for him. He had to consider the impact of his decisions on so many lives, amid heightened emotions and with an uncertain future.

Originally hailing from Scotland, Brown went from building Meccano and Lego models as a child, to building and managing remote power grids and stations during the day and working as a special police constable at night, to heading up Perth Airport. If you ask Brown, he'll tell you it's the culmination of all his life and career experiences that prepared him to lead through the pandemic – and that he was always up for the challenge.

I asked Brown how he stayed calm enough to get himself, his people and the organisation through it. He said, 'We already had a detailed pre-pandemic response before everything hit. Preparation erases doubt and breeds confidence. That's my go-to.'

At an innate level we can hear that Brown's approach to leading through adversity is to be *presilient*. He hadn't even heard of the term when I mentioned it to him; it was just second nature for him to think like that. 'You've got to be able to work well with your team and build your adaptive responses to the unknown piece by piece. There is no room for bureaucracy.' Brown's wise words have translated into enhanced service quality, strong profits for the airport and a jump in property value.

While we might not all go through experiences that signal Armageddon to our brains, the good news is that developing a pre-silient approach can grow through building the right mindset, and through practice. Pat Reed calls it 'acting yourself into a new way of thinking'.

And guess what? You are already halfway there, because the first step to becoming presilient is building the right mindset (which we have already started working on) to regulate your emotional thermostat. This is the *being* of presilience. Then you must learn how to implement it. That's where we're headed next: the *doing*.

## Reflection

· Waiting for the axe to drop in life and at work means always reacting to the fallout after situations have occurred, which can really take its toll. Can you think of a situation where being more on the offensive could have helped you be better prepared to navigate challenging events?

· Are you someone who plans for every potential scenario, or who responds more intuitively in the moment? How would listening to your instincts sooner and planning for the best and worst outcomes enable you to glide more effortlessly through the shocks and slides of business?

# CHAPTER 22

# PLANNING FOR THE UNKNOWN

A snake that you can see, does not bite.

– AFRICAN PROVERB

A few years ago I was speaking at an international risk conference and had the privilege of following George Jones on stage. Jones was the former chairman of Sundance Resources: an international iron-ore company headquartered in Western Australia, with assets located in central West Africa.

The company made the headlines in 2010 when all of its directors, and some of its officers and other staff, were killed in a plane crash in the Republic of Congo. As a result of the loss, the company halted its African operations and ordered staff to help find the plane. Trading of its shares was also put on hold. Since the incident the company, while still operating, was delisted from the Australian Stock Exchange in 2020 and has had a very low profile in the resources business community.

This is no doubt an unbelievably harrowing tale of loss and grief. But it's also an incredible situation for us to learn from.

When it came to question time after Jones' conference speech, there was only one thing I wanted to ask him – because hindsight is 20/20, right? I asked, 'What is one thing you know now that you wish you knew back then?'

His answer: 'I wish I had known I had to be better prepared for the unknown.'

Could Jones and the team have been better prepared for the unknown? Could the deaths have been avoided? The psychology of presilience and high performance says the loss could have been minimised, for sure.

Leaders with unreasonable ambition always think ahead and have specific behaviour strategies they adopt to reinforce their growth mindset and kickstart it into action. It's how they prepare for the future, even when they are in the midst of trouble.

## THE CRAFT OF NEGATIVE VISUALISATION

I hope by now I've convinced you that we need to commit to a 'default setting of presilience'.[63] But how exactly do we plan for the unknown?

*Negative visualisation* is one technique I use to help build presilience. It sounds confronting, doesn't it? It makes sense that it might, for a couple of reasons.

First, the benefits of positive visualisation to envisage our ideal life are more widely known.

Second, you may have heard about psychologists' use of a technique called 'exposure therapy' or 'systematic desensitisation' to help 'cure' people of their debilitating phobias via repeated exposure to the stimulus that is causing them terror. For example, a person with an obsessive fear of spiders (arachnophobia) might be treated by having repetitive exposure to spiders (yikes!). I have an irrational fear of clowns – coulrophobia – and get cold sweats and heart palpitations when I see them, so to be forced to confront them is a terrifying prospect!

And yet, engaging in a mental process of visualising all the worst-case scenarios that could go down in your life and at work is an extremely transformative mind hack. It helps you achieve true calm in anticipation of a tornado. Leaders with unreasonable ambition use it to better prepare themselves to deal with whatever storm is headed their way.

To practise negative visualisation, you start by brainstorming all the worst possible outcomes of a specific situation that causes you stress or anxiety. You then act each one out repeatedly, teaching your brain with each 'performance' to become habitualised to the impending scenarios so it can calm itself down at the right moment. In this way you are training your brain to prepare itself to successfully deal with all potential eventualities.

The secret is to recreate the scenarios right down the last detail and not stop, no matter how uncomfortable it gets. Think of it as *mental scenario planning* to enable you to see the future and prepare your responses in advance through repetition.

The figure on the next page is a step-by-step guide.

I've used this technique with professional musicians and athletes. I once coached a talented violinist to prepare for a major performance by pre-creating, as closely as possible, the performance conditions – right down to the time of day, the clothes she'd wear and the chair she'd use. She imagined every unwanted scenario she could be confronted with on the night; anything that could distract her or thwart her from a knockout show. And her performance on the night was breathtaking!

| Presilience Implementation Plan |

| Pre-create the stressful situation down to the last detail | No stopping allowed | Repeat. Repeat. Again |

When I worked with a French Canadian pro golfer, we went to the course in Mont-Tremblant, Québec, where he was playing the game. Against a spectacular backdrop of snow-capped mountains, we played out all the scenarios that could possibly throw off his game: from the rustling of the spectators to the whistling of the wind blowing through the trees (we checked the weather conditions!) and the distant buzzing of a lawnmower in the distance. He nailed it on the day of the tournament and has gone on to become a highly respected player (he affectionately called me his 'Bagger Vance', which I was chuffed about).

Here's another example. Pierre was an unreasonably ambitious CIO of a billion-dollar export business I worked with out of Ottawa, Canada. He had an upcoming pitch to potential investors for a high-stakes opportunity, for which he was seeking investment funds. He was extremely nervous and lacking in confidence. To prepare Pierre I took him through the following steps:

- **Imagine:** Before the meeting, I asked Pierre to imagine all the possible scenarios that could go wrong and write them down.
- **Replay:** Then it was time to act out the scenarios one by one.
- **Plan the logistics:** Detail here is important. We got access to the room Pierre was having the meeting in to make sure the experience was as true to life as possible. This also enabled him

to position himself for maximum impact and influence during the presentation.

- **Dress up:** I asked Pierre to wear the clothes he would be wearing on the day. This ensured he was comfortable and looked his best in the presentation. What we wear and how we look can significantly impact our confidence levels. If we look good, we feel great!

- **Hear the sounds and see the visual cues:** I asked Pierre to imagine the hush of the boardroom and visualise the faces of the expectant people he would be presenting to. I asked him to do his research, confirm who was attending and find out what they looked like if he hadn't met them before, so he could imagine their faces.

- **Anticipate reactions:** The better you know the people in the room the easier it will be to anticipate their responses to the different scenarios. There were some attendees Pierre had limited knowledge of. I encouraged him to try to find someone who could provide insights to help him imagine what their reactions would be based on their personalities and motivations.

I also had a couple of extra tips to ensure success:

- **No stopping allowed:** There's no exit door until you complete the experience, no matter how uncomfortable. You must see it through.

- **Repeat, and repeat again:** The skill is in learning to endure and control spikes of intense emotion. Time and repetition are your best friends.

There is no question that taking yourself through this process can be daunting and requires courage. Yet the benefits of doing the hard work to mentally prepare for real-life possibilities and come up with tangible ways to cope with them outweighs the inevitable distress or failure you may experience if you don't.

Leaders with unreasonable ambition don't hesitate to build these internal stress tests and contingency plans for potential risks with significant consequences, because they know how much this thinking can benefit them.

By the way, you might be curious to know how Pierre went. He was not successful in attaining the funding the first time. But what's important is how he recovered in the moment and that it invigorated his motivation to go back into the ring for another round.

## PREPARING FOR THE FUTURE THAT YOU WANT

There is no crystal ball to enable any of us to predict what is coming with 100 per cent accuracy.

What we *do* have control over is how we prepare our mindset so we can overcome highly pressurised situations – instead of just trying to get through and endure them – the *being* of presilience. It's about committing to moving your presilience mindset into autopilot.

Unreasonably ambitious leaders take advantage of the change that is happening around them so they can better adapt to and thrive in new environments and situations as they emerge. In turn, the *doing* of presilience creates a real-time learning loop for them to shape their desired future and invent novel ways to create it with every iteration.

How are you feeling right now? A little nervous? Perhaps a tad excited about trying on these techniques to get yourself in an accelerated flow state?

Experiencing a whole gamut of emotions is completely normal. It's likely that, for some of you, this material has sparked some deep self-reflection. Perhaps it has highlighted moments where you surpassed your own expectations of yourself, or maybe could have handled something better? I want you to be kind to yourself, no matter what. We are all on our own unique quest in life. Unreasonably ambitious leaders are on a lifelong mission to be the best version of themselves every day. Their aim is to position themselves, their teams and their businesses to adapt, innovate and improve wherever possible.

Coming up in challenge 6 we are going to focus more on the *doing*: boosting your presilience muscle with techniques to lift your performance to hyperspeed, even in the face of enormous distractions, extreme turbulence and uncertainty. I'll leave you with a couple of questions to ponder.

## Reflection

- Think about what might have happened if George Jones and his team at Sundance had gone through this process before getting on the plane to Africa. What decisions might have been made differently if they'd engaged their presilience nous to plan out their trip? Would it have made a difference to the outcome?

# CHALLENGE 6

# SUPERCHARGING YOUR PRODUCTIVITY

Light can devour the darkness but darkness
cannot consume the light.

– KEN POIROT

Throughout my career I have been privileged to work with the most extraordinary people creating societal change in quiet and spectacular ways. In this book, I didn't only want to write about the lives of the rich and famous. I wanted to pay homage to all the others: the unknown heroes making a difference in the world. These are the people you may never hear about but are equally worthy of mention – the *angels among us*.

When I worked with the Red Cross in Ottawa at the end of the war in former Yugoslavia, my role was to assist in the selection of relief workers who would travel to the war-torn country to bring home any remaining casualties' bodies. My work saw me researching and devising a personality profile for the type of person who could do this job successfully, without becoming mentally incapacitated by it. I must have interviewed more than 100 people to be able to ascertain the psychological makeup of those who would be best suited to and survive this type of work.

I was enthralled by what I discovered. I found that the most psychologically equipped minds were those that were able to deafen the noise of their emotional reactions to often terrifying visual stimuli (such as death and devastation) and focus on a singular purpose: establishing the identities of the fallen.

You may be wondering why I am using such a confronting example to illustrate how to supercharge your productivity. It's because, while the context is different, the conditions are scarily similar to what we are all experiencing right now: an ever-demanding life on hyperspeed, with our psychological reactions comparable to those we might experience in a country rocked by conflict.

The learning was in seeing how these individuals sent 'into battle' navigated environments that would bring most people to their knees. I discovered what made these humans extraordinary: a particular set of enhanced skills that translated into a winning performance on the ground. They were skills that one might expect to see in a triage nurse working the graveyard shift in the emergency department of a major hospital – cool, calm control, surging energy and focus, supercharged decision-making and organisation skills enabling military-precision execution.

In the following chapters I am going to break down this suite of psychologically defining skills and techniques. They result in a steeliness of mind that can be sustained even in the most harrowing of circumstances, without losing your life in the process.

You've already heard me speak a lot about how to prepare your mind to become calm in the eye of the storm (the *being* of presilience). But how do you translate this into the *doing* – where you're teetering on the cusp of your high-performance zone, ready to take action?

The three key methods we are going to unpack are:

1.  Learning to welcome distractions and get busy, putting your mind and hands to work.
2.  Decluttering your life to support high-performance habits.
3.  Freeing up your mind to burn rubber on the track and win the race.

Who's ready to power up their productivity?

# CHAPTER 23

# THE BENEFITS OF DISTRACTION

All that is gold does not glitter,
Not all those who wander are lost.

– JRR TOLKIEN

Let's face it: distraction is a dirty word these days. We're barraged with a steady stream of messaging telling us we must manage our many distractions if we're to be respected, perform and produce. We have been brainwashed into believing that distractions are evil.

With dramatic spikes in diagnoses of neurological disorders such as ADD and ADHD, there is even more of a paranoid focus on the perils of distractibility and the inevitable failure associated with being a busy manager.[64]

But what if I told you that being busy can also be good for your mental health, and that it's a great way to remain calm when you're caught in the eye of the storm?

Contrary to what you might have heard from self-help gurus, there exists a mass of neuroscientific research that reports on the many surprising benefits that come with keeping busy. Did you know that the single most important goal for people who are traumatised is to stay busy and work more? We are happier when we are busy!

It's not really that hard to believe, is it? Think about a time when you have been stressed out to the max or you've been hit with an unexpected situation, possibly a crisis you were not prepared for but one that required you to act quickly.

There are two typical reactions. You may have shut down and been paralysed by fear, and unable to make decisions. Or you might have stayed calm and launched quickly into action, moving heaven and earth to turn a dire situation around. If that's you, you're able to move to a state of calm much more quickly than the shut-down person.

Completing the tasks required to resolve a challenge creates a kind of hyperfocus and heightened mental acuity, even in the midst of a tornado. It's the same intense *busyness* that has driven so many 'underperforming' teams I have worked with over the years to rise and deliver impressive collective feats of ingenuity and resolution during times of crisis. Somehow, no matter how dysfunctional they may have been, in those moments they manage to unite around a burning platform and get super focused, busy and efficient. It's as if 'the hands are forcing order on the mind'.[65]

The psychology on this is clear. Emotional stress is managed in a couple of ways by our minds – by *avoiding it* or by *facing it* (you'll remember how I have been encouraging you to make friends with your stress).

Avoiding emotional distress by distracting yourself from it – the technique we hear less about – can equally serve a valuable role in the right circumstances.

In the example I gave above, when teams can step into the fire with the bravery and resolve to turn things around through a focus on task completion, they are able to make better decisions and execute faster. This simple workplace example flips being busy on its head, proposing that instead of spending all our time trying to manage our distractions, we need to make better use of the benefits that being busy brings.

Remember George Jones, former chairman of Sundance Resources, who we met in chapter 22? He said that, as they sought to guide the rest of the organisation through the shock of what happened, he instructed staff to get back to work. He said: 'I knew that it sounded callous, but I figured being busy was the best way to help people process what has happened until I could figure out my next move.'

Jones was on to something. The abundance of research on the benefits of busy hands and minds reveals myriad advantages, including increasing energy, motivation, productivity and creative thinking. It's also great for your brain health, boosts mental alertness and is an excellent way to cope with stress.

## LET YOUR MIND WANDER

I can't help reflecting on how my daydreaming habit as a child helped me get through some tough moments (while irritating the hell out of my mother, Penelope). She'd often catch me staring into space, looking out my bedroom window. 'Vanessa is quite ethereal,' she'd tell people, trying to fathom who this otherworldly child was.

Reconceptualising daydreaming as a high-performance habit flies in the face of societal norms. The truth is, the joy I experienced from letting my mind wander helped me navigate the complexities and trauma of my childhood. It provided me with the mental space to be able to quieten down any surging stress responses, and reframe my thoughts into clear and positive pathways to action. The verdict is clear on this. People who allow their minds to drift off are happier, and experience greater success at work. It is time to lose the guilts around your own daydreaming and own it as a superpower.[66]

**People who allow their minds to drift off are happier, and experience greater success at work.**

Just as I was able to distract my attention away from emotions that had the potential to cripple me, the Red Cross workers I mentioned earlier were able to compartmentalise their reactions to the devastation around them – so they could prioritise work and get the job done.

## PRODUCTIVITY IS AN ENDURANCE SPORT FOR THE MIND

You may be thinking I am being negligent right now. How could an organisational psychologist encourage you to engage in intentional distraction and busyness as an effective way to deal with heightened stress triggers?

Because that is exactly it: it's a technique to help you get through intensely turbulent experiences. You will still need to work through the emotions you have temporarily put on hold later (those emotions aren't going anywhere!).

Unreasonably ambitious leaders are committed to maintaining a healthy mind so that they can last the distance and make it back from the other side. Think of this as giving your psyche a raincheck until you have dealt with the immediate threat.

Andrew Broad, a serial CEO and resources executive, is a grounded leader who has achieved extraordinary success in his life. A country boy at heart, Broad decompresses by hooning around his property in the Perth Hills on his Kubota lawnmower. It helps him stay centred and get clarity on his big decisions. He is one of the calmest leaders I know!

What's another way we can make sure we are operating from a place of productivity rather than panic? By being freakishly well organised. In chapter 24 we will explore how planning and organisation is critical to sustaining high performance and enabling faster decision-making.

## Reflection

- Are you able to enjoy downtime without experiencing feelings of guilt?

- How do you view others who daydream?

- How do you manage your time out to carve mental space for creating?

- What activities or support do you seek out to keep your mind healthy?

# CHAPTER 24

# MARIE KONDO YOUR MIND

From the moment you start tidying, you will be compelled to reset your life. As a result, your life will start to change. That's why the task of putting your house in order should be done quickly. It allows you to confront the issues that are really important. Tidying is just a tool, not the final destination.

– MARIE KONDO

No-one would have predicted that in 2014 a pixie-like Japanese woman by the name of Marie Kondo would become a *New York Times* bestseller, build an empire out of her organisational skills and become the world's most famous declutterer. Her first book, *The Life-Changing Magic of Tidying Up*, sold over 1.5 million copies. The second, *Spark Joy*, published two years later, sold a whopping 11 million copies in 40 countries.[67]

You may be wondering what an obsessive desire to purge your cupboards has to do with unreasonably ambitious leadership. Well, it's this: being able to think straight during times of information overload requires a mind that is well organised. An organised mind helps to bring method to the madness amid the spill of ideas and thought bubbles. Unreasonably ambitious leaders have figured out how to bring order and stability to the people and organisations they serve, without sacrificing the speed required to deliver results quickly and stay on top of their game. They have developed the ability to ruthlessly prioritise and focus the attention of collective efforts on what matters most – on what creates value.

> **They have developed the ability to ruthlessly prioritise and focus the attention of collective efforts on what matters most.**

We talked earlier about the extraordinary benefits that come from *preactive planning* (an attempt to predict the future and then plan for that predicted future), and relying on your newly formed presilience muscle to make better decisions about likely outcomes.

Unreasonably ambitious leaders go one step further. Once they have predicted the future, they *proactively plan* for it. They mobilise their troops to take advantage of change; they *adapt and thrive in the new environment*. To do this requires them to 'declutter' their organisations. They must reorganise structures, processes and workflows so they can focus only on the essential, and eliminate the expendable.

The highly ordered mind can do anything when it stops trying to do everything. (Multitasking is *not* the hallmark of an unreasonably ambitious leader. Did you know multitasking diminishes the accuracy and quality of your decisions and efforts?)

---

**The highly ordered mind can do anything when it stops trying to do everything.**

---

In this way, unreasonably ambitious leaders actively shape their future rather than just trying to get ahead of events outside of their control. They decide what success looks like and make decisions about what to stop, what to change and what to leave as is (for now). This enables them to focus collective energy in the desired direction and accelerate the organisation's agility to realise it.

Once we have leveraged our distractions to direct focused energy to our top priorities, and organised our environment to support our efforts, we create a springboard to accelerate our decision-making. In the high-stakes world of global business, those who succeed are usually operating at a very fast pace. Being able to make high-velocity decisions, learn fast when they go wrong and keep up with the pace of change is what enables unreasonably ambitious leaders to outrun their competition and get the edge.

Satya Nadella was able to turn Microsoft into a learning organisation that recovered quickly from daily, inevitable failures. He accelerated the speed of decision-making to corner the market and make the necessary pivots during the upheaval of stock fluctuations. He essentially Marie Kondoed Microsoft to get leaders to focus their efforts on what mattered most to transform the organisation, and nothing else.

So, what's next? You've got your world in order. Your shoes are on, you can see the path and you've moblilised your troops. You're ready to start sprinting towards new horizons.

Let's go.

## Reflection

· What's your mental process for prioritising your attention and efforts?

· What gets in the way of you letting go of people, processes and practices that are stopping you from progressing?

· How do you balance agility, speed and accuracy?

# CHAPTER 25

# DRIVE LIKE A FERRARI

I feel the need, the need for speed.

– MAVERICK, *TOP GUN*

Unreasonably ambitious leaders are fast decision-makers and quick to execute.

In the wake of a future characterised by disruption, complication and uncertainty, being able to take control of your mind, quash your reptilian brain's need for certainty and execute swiftly is the epitome of adaptability in action. But valuing speed over perfection is a new habit to build. It's a habit of the unreasonably ambitious that we need to install into our new operating system.

It feels as if, almost overnight, we've moved on from a relatively stable and predictable world where perfectionism and getting things right were recognised as must-have attributes of a successful leader. Now, perfectionistic tendencies are recognised as *enemies of adaptability*. But here's the tricky part: you've probably been promoted because of your high standards and been publicly celebrated for them, which makes perfection a very hard habit to break.

And yet, redefining what 'done' looks like is necessary if you want to succeed in TUNA (turbulent, uncertain, novel and ambiguous) times.[68] Where once security and predictability were valued, flexibility and chaos now dominate. So, a continued focus on attaining perfection, the quality that once set you apart from others, has now become one of your greatest *liabilities*.

This is why technical leaders and organisations are struggling more than most to step into new frontiers, build their capacity to learn on the fly and throw out the rulebook for a future that is emerging right in front of their eyes. Reaching into your old bag of tricks to pull out something that worked in the past simply won't cut it any more, because 'inventiveness is not spurred on by relying on past solutions'.[69]

Cast your mind back to the Red Cross relief workers we met in challenge 6. They were tasked with making rapid decisions with limited information. This required them to rely on 'two brains running' to 'think fast and slow' (as psychologist Daniel Kahneman says) – the combination of a high-speed intuitive, emotional brain and a slower, rational brain to make a swift judgement call under fire.[70]

Dr Michael Ryan, executive director of the World Health Organization's Health Emergencies Programme, has been on the frontline of several world health threats of late. He says, 'If you need to be right before you move, you will lose. Speed trumps perfection. Perfection is the enemy of good when it comes to emergency management.'[71]

We have already explored several techniques to kickstart your mental agility when your hard wiring is screaming at you to stop and stay the same. Fighting against a biology that is not naturally built for rapid change is your greatest hurdle. The good news is that agility is completely learnable.

Unreasonably ambitious leaders are able to move their mindsets into a place where they jump headfirst into the messy puddle of imperfection, making decisions on the fly whether they work or not.

Let me explain how they do it.

## DRIVING FAST

I'm certain you met this person before. The leader who takes forever to get back to you (if they do at all). The manager who fails to intervene when there is a toxic staff issue. The ditherer who waffles their way through meetings; meetings that are as boring as watching paint dry and feel like groundhog day. These leaders tend to stay quiet when decisions need to be made; or they defer to others, acting in the guise of 'democracy' to stall on decisions they don't have the guts to make.

Indecisiveness is one of those career-ending qualities that can quickly cause leaders to lose their troops' respect. It leaves everybody wondering whose palms this person greased to even get a shot at the leadership guernsey in the first place!

In a world where we are barraged with information, being able to filter through it and get the right input is the first step to setting yourself up for faster decision-making. Unreasonably ambitious leaders *act quickly on the information they have*, relying on their improvisation skills to pirouette their way across the stage of ambiguity with more than one dance move at the ready.

Unreasonably ambitious leaders act quickly on the information they have.

Someone who immediately pops into my mind is Kevin Gallagher, CEO of Australian-based energy company Santos. I first heard about Gallagher when I was chatting with Harold Clough who, at 93 years of age, wanted to explore his legacy (but that's a cool story for another time!). I had asked Clough who he thought was a great leader and he gave me a few names; Gallagher's was right up there at the top of his list. So, I reached out to Gallagher to find out what had made Clough, an iconic business pioneer, so excited and brimming with pride.

Before meeting Gallagher, I learned that during his time at the helm he had successfully led his organisation to gain competitive edge through the energy transition. Steered by his leadership, this very traditional organisation had been rebuilt from the ground up. Today, the company is proudly holding a position in the ASX-20 and has been ranked as one of the top 20 energy businesses globally.

These are outstanding results, no doubt; but it's the unreasonably ambitious leader behind the wheel, and the story of how he dragged his organisation kicking and screaming into the new world order, that is the real gold. Gallagher found a way against the odds and non-believers, and I wanted to find out how.

What struck me about Gallagher at our first encounter was his natural charisma and sense of mirth. He is serious and playful, demanding and curious. With intense eyes so blue they are disconcerting, Gallagher is not someone you forget. Excitable, incorrigible, buzzing with electricity and raging in his insatiable hunger for progress, his ambitions are palpable, his conviction contagious. As I sat opposite him my mind conjured up the image of a racehorse at the gate, ready to bolt. I imagined that anyone working with him would have to make a choice: either jump on his back and hang on for the ride or fall off and be left behind in the dirt.

Like so many unreasonably ambitious leaders, Gallagher relies heavily on his ability to scan for patterns in his external environment and translate this sense-making into new insights and potential plays in the market. Clearly, his ability to make great decisions about how to realise his insights have resulted in mind-blowing gains for his organisation. But capitalising on his strategic foresight to make future decisions would not have led to windfall returns if he hadn't matched it with high-quality data and a penchant for taking fast action.

Interestingly, this is where I see many leaders become blocked, stuck in the slow lane with a clear vision and direction but drowning in the details.

Gallagher is clever enough to validate his instincts with high-quality input, then move quickly from validation to action without getting stuck in a sticky web of procrastination.

Gallagher's story showcases how *leading agile is a balancing act*. To unlock your organisation's full potential you must be able to calibrate its need for both *stability* and *speed*. They are two sides of the same coin.

Here are a couple of simple yet powerful questions I like to ask leaders when they are in danger of not moving fast enough:

- **What does 'done' look like?** This gives a clear picture of success based on current data and information.
- **Is it good enough for now?** This enables leaders to move from idea to adaptive action quickly, rather than chasing their perfectionistic tails.

The 40:70 rule is another tool I like to use to help leaders sense-check their thinking before taking action.

## THE 40:70 RULE

The 40:70 rule is specific to decision-making and useful in making tough calls in the heat of the moment. It's also a strong capability I see in the unreasonably ambitious.

The rule was originally proposed by Colin Powell, former US Secretary of State. His view was that successful CEOs need to make a call when they have between 40 and 70 per cent of the information available. Less than 40 per cent of the right information is like 'shooting from the hip' and likely to result in poor decision quality; waiting for more than 70 per cent will 'delay the decision' unnecessarily.[72]

The key here is to adopt a learning mindset and be prepared to explore what's possible. Unreasonably ambitious leaders like Gallagher tend to intentionally frame future challenges by acknowledging that they don't have all the answers, but they're confident that they will be able to figure it out: 'I don't know what it looks like, but I will be ready to tackle it with a bit more information.' Sound familiar? Remember how we defined 'delusional' earlier on?

The power of this thinking is commendable. Gallagher came from a background of getting things right. The entire trajectory of his career progression was rooted in perfection and black-and-white solutions. If his previous habits had taken hold, he would have been held back from greater possibilities.

At a deeper level, you can see how in a wobbly world where uncertainty is a given, operating from an ego-driven mindset of perfectionism would result in the stifling of progress. Unreasonably ambitious leaders like Gallagher have learned to reason with Socratic thinking: 'The only thing I know is that I know nothing.'

Once you've made the decisions and move to action, how much time do you spend on execution? Where is the best place to focus your energy?

Steve Jobs said, 'We're always thinking about new markets we could enter, but it's only by saying no that you can concentrate on the things that are really important.'

Touché!

Agile and transformation guru Pat Reed has a very practical strategic decision-making litmus test she uses. The test ensures leaders are focused on making decisions that yield the greatest value, and balance the interplay of agility (flexibility and speed) and stability (rigour and scale). She told me: 'You need to spend about 60 per cent of your time delivering on your core function, your main business. Then about 30 per cent on continuous improvement and building innovation as a company-wide capability. The last 10 per cent is time spent purely on upskilling and learning.'

## THE ROLE OF TECHNOLOGY AND SYSTEMS

It would be remiss of me not to address the glaring void in my ramblings at this point. Traditional organisations such as Santos are at a tipping point in their evolution where their ability to compete in a disrupted world will hinge primarily on how fast they can adapt and 'learn faster than everybody else'.[73]

In addition to having access to high-quality data and acting quicky on it by taking a 'test and learn' approach to problem-solving, we cannot underestimate the unparalleled advantage that organisational culture, technology and systems provide to speed up and empower better decision-making.

Hierarchical structures, sluggish organisational processes and command-and-control cultures are the greatest barriers to fast action. As one executive said, 'You need to kill and hide bureaucracy... fast decision-making means fewer signatures.'[74]

Personally, I like to ask my clients to name the dumbest things they do, and then ask them to prepare to throw them all out! Blowing up antiquated ways of operating takes unreasonable ambition; you must be prepared to acknowledge what's not working, and be brave enough to ditch stuff and move forward with the future in mind.

But sometimes it's hard to maintain a can-do attitude when things are hairy and going off the rails in life and at work. What's another tip for hanging in there?

In challenge 7: unreasonable thinking we will explore the lighter side of building an unreasonably ambitious mindset by helping you find the fun in adversity, maintain perspective when things seem insurmountable and embrace your humanity, warts and all.

Let's switch our focus to a brighter side of life.

## Reflection

- If I gave you a magic wand that would enable you to make something disappear that is getting in the way of your success at work, without consequence, what would it be?

- What factors come into play to set your success and kill criteria for your projects and decisions?

- How do you know when you're done?

## CHALLENGE 7

# UNREASONABLE THINKING

When she transformed into a butterfly, the caterpillars spoke not of her beauty, but of her weirdness. They wanted her to change back into what she always had been. But she had wings.

– DEAN JACKSON

I think you're getting the gist of it: *transformation is an inside job*.

Steve Jobs' reflection on this is so apropos. He said, 'If you want to live your life in a creative way, as an artist, you have to not look back too much. You have to be willing to take whatever you've done and whoever you were and throw them away.'

No matter your opinion on Jobs and his leadership, his commitment to continually disrupting himself and his business is undeniable. It's what made him hard to look away from.

Everyone has the potential to be a rockstar. It's not a right reserved for the rich and famous or the certifiable. But to get there takes a lifelong commitment to cultivating the right state of mind. Even in those moments when your life feels bleak and your efforts seem pointless, you've got to be able to tap into your well of potential and awaken that sleeping giant to start roaring and wreak positive turbulence on the world. You have to be desperate to make your mark.

## Everyone has the potential to be a rockstar.

Dr Jodie Forlonge is an unreasonably ambitious leader I heard speak at a Perth networking event. She's a remarkable woman who's made a career of busting through archaic gender stereotypes and a deeply rooted patriarchy to realise some big and audacious life goals.

From a young age Forlonge wanted to fly. She spent 20 years in the Australian Defence Force, cracking the concrete ceiling to become an army major (only 40 per cent of recruits make it in!) and flying Black Hawk helicopters in areas of conflict and war. This was her path before calling it quits and jumping into medicine a couple of decades later.

What struck me about Forlonge was her open demeanour, down-to-earth attitude and the sheer force of her determination to live life on her terms. Her dream of becoming a doctor had started back in high school in Kingscliff, northern New South Wales. Even the onslaught of comments from people thinking she was crazy to go back to university didn't dissuade her from doing it. She always knew it would happen.

Is this sounding familiar? What is it with all these non-believers?!

What's so interesting about Forlonge's career trajectory is her attraction to not one but two high-adrenaline occupations. For Forlonge, life is an adventure to be explored, and it's worth taking the risks to chase it.

But what is it that helps her keep her sanity in check and maintain high performance and mental sharpness during heightened stress, when life is on the line? How does she motivate herself to strive for and achieve so many big, hairy goals?

'I love to have fun!' she told us. 'When I was in the army and we were about to deploy into war-torn countries, doing practical jokes helped me deal with high-pressure situations. I remember this one time I was having my period so I set up a bear trap outside my room to warn people that I was not feeling all that sociable and they should enter at their own risk. You know, because bears are attracted to blood!'

Diffusing the intensity of an impending tough situation has always been Forlonge's go-to. As inappropriate as she may sound (which I celebrate, by the way!), Forlonge is on to something. Being able to tap into your inner child and be a bit of a prankster is a well-documented technique to relieve stress, quickly put yourself into a great state of mind and strengthen your relationships; not to mention create lasting moments of joy.

Unreasonably ambitious leaders don't tend to take themselves too seriously. Even when the world is on fire, they choose their attitude and their responses to it just like Forlonge. And it keeps them going, against all odds, in pursuit of an endless summer.

In the next few chapters, we are going take a walk on the lighter side of *unreasonable ambition*. First let's focus on exploring how committing to a life of play can lead to miraculous outcomes (I am not joking!). Perspective is everything, and being able to stay humble and maintain a grounded perspective sets you up to confidently wrestle even the most ferocious of bears entering your campground.

We're going to finish up with creativity. It is my innate belief that all human beings are creative. Being able to tap into your inner artist is key to accessing unconstrained thinking, generating new knowledge and solving complex future challenges with a heightened level of mastery.

Now, let's go have fun!

# CHAPTER 26

# FINDING THE FUN IN ADVERSITY

Play keeps us vital and alive. It gives us an enthusiasm for life that is irreplaceable. Without it, life just doesn't taste good.

– LUCIA CAPOCCHIONE

Have you heard the story of Joe Simpson and Simon Yates? Simpson wrote a book that was turned into a heart-racing, cliffhanger movie called *Touching the Void* (2003). The movie tells the story of how Simpson survived an almost fatal mountaineering accident in 1985. He and his friend, Yates, had just reached the peak of a 21,000-foot mountain in the Peruvian Andes when he slipped and fell 150 feet into a deep crevasse, shattering his leg and foot 'like marbles in a sock'.[75] Attached to his friend only by a 45-metre rope, and separated by darkness with no way of communicating, Yates cut the rope, sending Simpson plunging to certain death. But Simpson didn't die, and the story of how he survived is one of mountaineering's greatest survival tales.

Simpson managed to extricate himself from the crevasse by setting himself small time-based challenges to keep him moving towards freedom. He finally managed to hoist himself out and hop on one leg all the way down the mountain *'as if it were a dance'*. What makes Simpson's story so mesmerising is his mindset. His conscious decision to treat his extreme adversity as a game, with survival as the sweepstakes, is what ultimately saved Simpson from extinction. He was barely alive when he finally reached basecamp three days later.

Neuroscientists have their finger on the pulse in unpacking this one. It's a well-known fact that unreasonably ambitious people take great joy even from the smallest of wins. It's an important step in creating an ongoing feeling of motivation and preventing the descent into hopelessness. With this mindset they feel like they are making progress despite the huge challenges that confront them.

**Unreasonably ambitious people take great joy even from the smallest of wins.**

In chapter 6 we met former pro swimmer Dom Sheldrick. He told me about a similar mental strategy he used in training to win the gold medal while battling leukaemia. Like Joe he focused on breaking down his big goal of winning the gold into smaller, bite-sized goals that he was able to manage daily. By knocking these off one by one he didn't become overwhelmed by the enormity of the challenge that lay before him.

In doing so, both guys were able to tap into the particular mental reward centres in the brain that are often associated with playing games; the same centres stimulated when taking cocaine. Being able to turn a stressful situation or impossible goal into a game with stakes, challenges and little rewards can trick your psyche into a more positive state of mind. In both cases, it made miracles happen.

For Simpson it was survival. For Sheldrick it was surviving cancer and becoming a father to four children, even after battling leukaemia (he told me he imagined his nether regions encased in a leaden box to protect himself from infertility during chemotherapy!). Treating adversity as a game and playing to win is one of the most powerful mind hacks ever.

Thankfully, we are not all faced with life-or-death survival situations. An everyday work challenge that comes up for many clients in my leadership practice is looking for a new job after they have been laid off, made redundant or chosen to leave their employer. It's a stressful time for most as they sit in career limbo, hoping to transition quickly into a new and more exciting opportunity.

A little mind game I play with them, to get them motivated and focused on enjoying the liminal space and remaining productive, is to check in on how many jobs they are applying for daily. I might ask, 'How many résumés did you send off today? Can you beat yesterday's quota?'. It's amazing how a simple cognitive reframe like this speeds up their success, helping them land a new role much faster and with a more positive frame of mind.

## THE POWER OF PLAY

In the serious world of business, is there a place for playing and having fun?

It feels counterintuitive, but encouraging leaders to play and have fun, particularly in the wake of a global pandemic and economic upheaval, is a power tool for sustainable leadership success. Vast amounts of psychological research prove that the benefits of play are not just limited to children. Research points to the important role fun has in the workplace, offsetting the impact of prolonged stress. It's also been identified as a critical accelerator of creativity and lateral thinking, elevating cognitive functioning and helping us to solve wicked, complex problems faster.

Play is also the secret to a healthier life. In her book, *The Power of Fun: How to Feel Alive Again*, journalist and screen–life balance expert Catherine Price argues persuasively that 'true fun' (fun is a feeling, not an activity, she explains) is 'the magical confluence of playfulness, connection, and flow' that enables us to thrive and be energised.[76] Price's research has proven how having everyday moments of fun can launch you into longer states of high performance and better-quality relationships through deeper and more meaningful connections. It can also be a powerful health intervention (it's a resilience and growth-mindset booster!).

**Everyday moments of fun can launch you into longer states of high performance and better-quality relationships.**

Play is also a key driver of enhanced learning outcomes for adults. It's why you may have noticed an increased use of Lego Serious Play in leadership development and training sessions to stimulate curiosity and outside-the-box thinking. I've been using it for years, particularly when I am facilitating business strategy, to help flip participants' minds into a creative zone and enable blue-sky thinking. The results have been remarkable, and the energy created from my approach instrumental in birthing bold and colourful ideas to inform future plays.

The psychology on this speaks volumes. Joe Simpson's ability to trick his brain into thinking his harrowing fight to survive was a game to be played illustrates the potential of intentional play. More broadly it emphasises the upside of fostering fun cultures at work to create learning environments that spark ingenuity, even in the face of the seemingly insurmountable. The dopamine elicited by shared fun experiences helps teams and individuals make sense of and generate new ideas, and strengthen new memories. Fun fact: dopamine helps to stimulate the neural activity that correlates with creative thinking.

The vast benefits of using play and fun to help us turn around tough situations is not a new revelation. Legendary father of psychology Abraham Maslow acknowledged the fundamental role that play has in eliciting new insights, and as a key stepping stone to self-actualisation (that's a fancy word for reaching your full potential). He said, 'Almost all creativity involves purposeful play.' Note the use of the word 'purposeful'.[77]

So, if Maslow has been talking about it since 1968, you may wondering why I am stating the obvious? It's because, while many of us instinctively get this, few leaders are focused on actively pursuing play or treating it as a top priority in the all-too-serious world of work (except the unreasonably ambitious, of course!). Instead, we apologise for taking time off to play or feel guilty when we do. And yet, play is a drug-free antidote to a stress-riddled life, and a sure-fire way to inject a huge bolt of sunshine into your everyday experiences at home and at work.

---

**Play is a drug-free antidote to a stress-riddled life.**

---

I don't have enough fingers to count how many of the unreasonably ambitious leaders in my network tell me about their Fridays reserved just for golf (if they're not travelling, of course). You should see them light up like Christmas trees when they describe this! Their whole demeanour changes. It's such a joy to witness!

## Reflection

· How do you incorporate moments of play in your day?

· What do you do to foster fun at work?

## COMMIT TO HAVING MORE FUN

I'd like to conclude this chapter with a few simple yet stellar tips from Catherine Price on how to incorporate more fun in your day:

- **Leave your phone in a drawer:** Reduce the distractions that kick you out of flow by setting firm boundaries around your screen time. Price is a huge advocate of mindful tech disconnection to be more present and enjoy the fullness of experiences.
- **Hang out with people:** Research shows that the happiest memories of fun times usually involve other people.
- **Look for moments to go against the grain:** Engaging in what Price calls 'playful deviance' to break the responsibilities of adulthood is a way to boost feelings of joy. An example might be going to a movie with friends in the middle of the day with a hip flask for a sneaky tipple. (I'm not advocating for the use of alcohol for stress relief; sometimes it's just fun to do something naughty!)
- **Put it at the top of the list:** Carve out the time to do the things that bring you joy.[78]

Now that I've got you into a playful headspace, I want to focus on the benefits of experiencing *sunshine from the inside*, from cherishing all the moments rather than letting life pass you by.

In the next chapter we'll explore how the way you interpret events and view the world and your place in it significantly impacts your happiness and how successful you become. We'll also look into the benefits of developing a more curious and humble perspective to be able to navigate life in all its permutations with clarity, confidence, compassion and gratitude.

# CHAPTER 27

# PERSPECTIVE IS EVERYTHING

Everything has beauty, but not everyone sees it.

– CONFUCIUS

Five years ago, my perspective on life changed forever.

I had just launched a new life entrepreneurship program, Trail-Blazer, for unreasonably ambitious female leaders. My then-business partner called me to have a serious chat. It was unusual for her to be so solemn, so I was intrigued as to what she wanted to speak to me about.

'So, I have found a person who is perfect for Trail-Blazer,' she said.

'Okay, great,' I replied. 'Tell me about her.'

She paused. 'Well, I need you to keep an open mind.'

At this point I was wondering what was about to come out of her mouth. I am nothing if not open, so the fact that she was preparing me had me a little on edge.

'Her name is Fiona. And she's ill.' Her words sounded like a lead balloon hitting a wooden floor.

'Sorry?' I asked incredulously. I thought I had misheard her.

'She's ill. She had a failed kidney transplant, and she is not going well.'

I didn't understand. Why would someone with a terminal condition want to do our program? There were so many questions and mixed emotions swirling inside me. How would she attend the program? What if something happened to her during a workshop? How would the other participants feel about having someone in the program who was suffering, and unwell? Would she feel uncomfortable? Would they feel uncomfortable?

My mind was racing. And then it hit me.

What an incredible gift to have Fiona in our program; for us to hear her perspective on life, love and work at this pivotal time in her life. And if there *was* discomfort, how fantastic! Real growth is always a bit awkward at the beginning. I couldn't wait to meet her.

When she walked into the room I was taken aback by her beauty. Dark-haired with classical Mediterranean features and swathed in a floral designer dress, she possessed an old-world elegance. She swept across the floor to greet me. Her energy was calm, ethereal, luminescent. It felt like a scene from a movie, in slow motion.

In her magical book *Phosphorescence*, journalist Julia Baird says human beings glow faintly even during the day; that the human body literally glimmers.[79] Baird asks:

> *Have you ever met someone in your life who just glowed from the inside? Someone who radiates goodness and seems to effortlessly emanate inner joy? A person who is so hungry for experience, so curious and engaged and fascinated with the world outside their head that they brim with life and light?*

These people are inspiring, they're magnetic, they're intoxicating, they're energising, they're strengthening.

That is Fiona.

I discovered that her life had been one long, crazy adventure from start to finish. She grew up on the poverty line, living with a father with mental illness; married one of the Portishead band members; and became a senior technology leader, managing digital transformation for one of the top mining companies in Australia.

Then one day, in 2015, she collapsed at work. She thought it was just a cold, only to discover she had renal failure. She told me how, during an interview she gave on ABC radio show *Drive* about the pilot for her new TV series *Thank you for Dying* (soon going into production in LA), journalist Geoff Hutchison asked her how she felt about getting her second chance at life.

'Well, your kidney took,' he declared.

'Oh,' she said in her ever-so-gracious way. 'No, it didn't.'

Radio silence.

'I'm still in kidney failure. I have about six to seven per cent of my kidney function.'

Kudos to Hutchison, who owned his assumption. 'Wow,' he said. 'I am looking at you, the picture of perfect health and assumed that just because you are sitting here smiling in front of me you were okay.'

He was floored.

'I can only go out for a couple of hours,' Fiona told him. 'But to do that I have to prepare and get myself ready.'

Talk about shifting his perspective in an instant!

Fiona's story gives us perspective in what it means to be mentally challenged to fight to stay alive. She is the perfect example of how an unreasonably ambitious leader makes sense of a life thrown into chaos.

'I don't think you're ever truly ready for this kind of fight,' Fiona told me. 'In the moments where I have been ready to give up, it's thinking about my organ donor who died for me to live that has kept me going. I owe it to him to fight the good fight.'

It is her hope that her side hustle, *Thank you for Dying,* will 'help people to deal with the new ordinary to do something beautiful with their lives'. She hopes it will raise awareness around the gift of organ donation, and how it gives people a second chance at life. 'It's a beautiful thing when a little piece of someone else becomes a part of you,' she says. 'I've got a short time to go do things, so I am not wasting it!'

What strikes me instantly when I am in the presence of unreasonably ambitious leaders like Fiona is how they can switch their perspective and go from a 'zero' situation to a 'hero' mindset so swiftly.

There is no doubt that Fiona's ability to stay the course has been amplified by her insatiable curiosity (she asks a lot of questions!), quirky sense of humour and self-effacing gratitude for life. These qualities also fuel her incredible talent as a creative innovator in her day job, and help her unlock creative potential in others. She's been leading the brand strategy and marketing for digital transformation service business idoba with CEO Sarah Coleman, helping them kick some serious goals as tech-informed mining industry disruptors – all from her bedside.

## THINKING BIG AND BEYOND

Perspective is the one thing that each one of us has that is unique from others. It is also one of the most powerful tools in building our relationships and expanding our worldview. But don't just take my word for it. In a study conducted by the USC Marshall Center for Effective Organizations it was found that 'the process of perspective-taking may be the most crucial communication process to an organization's success.'[80]

Psychologist Joscelyn Duffy describes it as 'the equivalent of seeing life as if through a tunnel and having someone break down the sides of the tunnel to create a more expansive perspective on life. Multiple perspectives are crucial to gain a full understanding of a concept, experience, or environment.'[81]

Let's steal a few moments to move our perspective into action. There are some key techniques I use with leaders to help build up their perspective-taking capabilities:

- **Understand your own unique view of the world:** We
  have all been on our own life journey. The culmination of
  all our experiences, absorption of messaging (conscious and
  unconscious), our relationships and our trials and tribulations
  have helped formed our views on life. Doing the work to
  understand what your views are is the first step in perspective-
  taking. As an example, this book that you are reading right now
  is a summation of decades of my unique lived experience and
  perspective on leadership. It may not resonate with you, or you
  may love it. Either way it's a perspective I am happy to share
  with you.

- **Seek first to understand:** Never assume anything. Assumption
  leads to conflict and gets in the way of tapping into alternate views
  and ideas. Adopting the mindset of a learner in all situations keeps
  you open and fluid. It also takes the pressure off when you let go
  of your ego and allow yourself to learn from others, knowing that
  *you do not know.*

- **Be present:** Give people the respect they deserve and stay in the
  moment. Not waiting for people to finish what they are saying
  before jumping in to speed up a meeting or say what you want
  to say robs you from expanding your mind with diverse ideas on
  the world. It's not great for your relationships, either. Don't fool
  yourself: people know when you're not listening.

- **Stay light:** Don't be so intense. Stay light and inquisitive. Come
  from a place of humble inquiry and focus on creating a fun and
  collaborative interchange that makes people want to open up.

If you're too serious and foreboding and it's a one-way monologue, it's boring. You want to get invited back to the party.

## Reflection

· How would you describe your own unique view of the world? What are some distinct and non-mainstream perspectives you hold on different topics that others would benefit from hearing about?

· How do you get yourself into a learning mindset that enables you to suspend judgement? Do you seek to understand another's narrative before jumping in with your own?

· What can you do to set yourself up to be fully present and in the moment?

· What's your energy like? What do you notice about your effect on other people's energy when you walk into the room? Are they happy to see you or do they look unenthused?

## KNOW YOUR PLACE

A while back I was travelling through Albuquerque, New Mexico. It's a spectacular place, with the contrast of the ochre sand and barren landscape against powder-blue skies and whirling pops of green spinifex that intermittently blow past.

I was in a serious relationship with a very clever Italian scientist who loved classic motorbikes and the great outdoors. We were hooning down a dusty road on the back of a vintage yellow Triumph motorbike, my hair streaming out the back of my helmet. I felt so alive and free as the wind rushed past us. We were going so fast; I couldn't see much. And then Las Mesas came into view. It's a Mars-like mountain range with an elevation of 2454 metres, and kilometres of smaller formations leading up to the main attraction. I asked my Italian companion to pull over. It was unlike any mountain I had ever seen. Red and craggy, it looked like a series of flattened tabletops holding up a limitless sky.

I was in awe.

In that moment, I felt my own insignificance. Standing in the shadows of this mighty monument of nature, me a speck of humanity at its doorstep.

I had a similar experience when I met Fiona for the first time. A shift in perspective can change your life forever.

Just as Mother Nature continues to inspire me daily, meeting Fiona helped me level up in big ways.

To reap the benefits of these awe-inspiring experiences, we have to notice, pay attention and be present. They demand openness and curiosity. It takes a willingness to stay small and remember our place in this world, committing to be better, every day.

Coming up in chapter 28 we will explore how to get your crazy on; how to create space to think big and beyond, and have the courage to stand alone – especially in the eye of the storm.

# CHAPTER 28

# THINKING BIG

If people aren't calling you crazy, you aren't thinking big enough.

– RICHARD BRANSON

I have rarely met an unreasonably ambitious leader who has not been called weird or crazy at some point in their life. In chapter 5 I spoke to the history of original thinkers and nonconformists and how they have been vilified and even burnt at the stake for thinking differently. And yet it's a side serve of crazy that we need to navigate today's unknown curveballs. We need more unconstrained and creative thinking to see around corners and reset the world order.

Innovation entrepreneur and serial rebel Jeff Melanson, who you met in chapter 14, believes the secret to reshaping the future of humanity lies in remembering our history as intrepid explorers. We must fully leverage our natural ability as human beings to conjure up things that never existed before. He says: 'For people who don't think agility and creativity is a requirement, I don't know what planet they think they are living on right now.'

For Melanson, creativity is a fundamental part of human brilliance. He believes that we are all endowed with the spirit of invention and capable of extraordinary acts of ingenuity, but that many of us discount our extreme capacity for creativity:

> Look around you. Everything that surrounds us is a product of our ingenuity, our ability as human beings to make things that did not exist before. It's a core capability that marks our evolution as a species. Being able to channel our innate creativity and reimagine worlds that don't exist yet is in our DNA.

Melanson reminds us that we are living in societies built by visionaries and dreamers, and people who were willing to take big, bold risks. He talks about how our societies, our countries and our individual lives would not be the way they are today had those who came before us decided that what was always done was the way things would be:

> If our ancestors had been attached to the way things were, we would still be living in caves and our lifespan would be 30 or less years. We need to stop honouring a legacy of what's come before us, by hanging onto past practices that no longer serve us. That is not legacy. Our legacy is our evolution.

## AGILITY IN UNEXPECTED PLACES

I am a big fan of unreasonably ambitious leader Bjarke Ingels, CEO of BIG. *Vogue* magazine recently named him the most sought-after architect in the world, reflecting his ability to consistently rebirth old buildings and structures while pumping out a steady course of innovation and magic.

He's also good mates with Melanson.

What's impressive about Ingels is his unconstrained thinking, his bold and brave future vision and his execution of the impossible. With Ingels, there are no limits. He is blowing up traditional notions of what's possible, from designing and building the new Lego HQ; to a ski hill in Denmark, run from the roof of the city's new ultra-green-waste-to-energy powerplant; to a reimagined pyramid in Manhattan; to his latest creation, Fuse Valley, the 'next Silicon Valley in Portugal'. To top it all off, he even teamed up with another modern-day revolutionary, Elon Musk, on the hyperloop project – an initiative that will likely transform human transportation forever.

His philosophy is rebellious, risqué and inspiring. He says:

> In a sense, being against something is almost being a follower in reverse. You always hear architects complaining about how their brilliant idea was watered down through compromise. My approach to architecture is really to try, in a Zen-like way, or like in aikido, to turn the force of your enemy into your own strength. By listening and observing and trying to accommodate the conditions we find, we arrive at something much more interesting.[82]

Ingels is an agile mindset in the flesh. He doesn't follow a set map or a plan, but flexes and morphs his builds as new data and insights emerge. He creates clever, category-defying feats of architectural genius while having fun:

> I like to use the idea of an architectural game of Twister. You start in a traditional pose, and then as you pile on demands, suddenly you find yourself in a back bend with your face rubbing up against the private parts of your family members, and it becomes enjoyable and fun. That's essentially what we're trying to do.

Cut of similar cloth to Ingels, another organisation that is upping the bar on what's possible is Moment Factory. Headed up by Dominic Audet, Sakchin Bessette and Éric Fournier of former Cirque du Soleil fame, its purpose is to bring people together by offering new experiences through multimedia 'to inspire a sense of collective wonder and connection'.

Moment Factory is forcing us to think differently about how we use public buildings and spaces, utilising them as semi-permanent canvases to create fully immersive and visually arresting digital entertainment experiences. Its creation of a 'Theatre of Experience' at Changi Airport, designed to enhance and entertain passengers at different stages of their journey, led to Singapore taking out the number-one spot for the best airport in the world for the fifth consecutive year.[83]

What is truly exciting about Moment Factory's work is how it uses technology to reimagine bridges, spaces and buildings to create a compelling sense of destination. The way it has adapted Cirque du Soleil's secret sauce to create a completely new, reconceptualised entertainment offering is also incredibly clever.

Think about it: two decades earlier, Cirque du Soleil co-founder Guy Laliberté reinvigorated a dying circus industry and created a whole new marketspace. He identified that people didn't want to see live animals being used in shows any more, and that children were more interested in playing video games than going to see circus tricks and juggling. To achieve his vision, he drew upon the distinctive strengths of other entertainment industries, such as theatre, Broadway shows and the opera, to offer a totally new experience for a more mature and higher-spending audience.

Supporting Cirque du Soleil through a time of evolution, what stood out for me was Laliberté's commitment to building a culture of courage and continuous exploration. He also deliberately stirred up a tension-filled environment, recognising that maintaining a degree of discomfort and ambiguity was the answer to sparking a creative edge in his people and his business.

And he was right. Remember how I suggested in chapter 10 you make friends with stress? Helping his people do that is a big part of

Laliberté's success. As a leader, he is always pushing the limits of his own thinking. His bold and brave mindset enabled him to short-circuit his own hardwiring and unlock the power of his organisation's creative potential. He helped people believe in magic again and in doing so invented a whole new industry.

> **He helped people believe in magic again and in doing so invented a whole new industry.**

Honouring its Cirque du Soleil origins, Moment Factory is a great example of a spin-off creative organisation that has built forward using its experiences and legacy. It preserved what worked well while unlocking inspiration to go much further creatively – showcasing its unbelievable agility in unexpected public spaces.

## WE ARE ALL CREATIVES

I hope I have convinced you of what human beings are capable of; what *you* are capable of: going towards your wildest dreams, beyond measure.

The renewed emphasis on creativity and critical thinking is reinventing the way problems are solved and business is done. It requires all of us to think bigger if we are to innovate and problem-solve for an uncertain future. It requires us to maximise the greatest human tools we have for accelerating agility, amplifying adaptation and sparking innovation in unexpected places to create breakthroughs for generations to come. As *Alice in Wonderland*'s Cheshire Cat said, 'Imagination is the only weapon in the war against reality.'

Your sleeping giant should be almost fully awake by now. But there is just one final tap of the magic wand left to make your giant jump to attention and move into action. Challenge 8: be selfless to be selfish is the most powerful challenge of all.

I have saved the best for last to end our adventure together on a life-changing high. We will explore techniques that help you focus your attention on things that fuel your heart and soul. And I am going to get really deep and emotional, really quick.

To equip you to control your mind and emotions, we'll also explore mind techniques that enable you to sit on the pinnacle of resilience and create a cycle of renewable energy; energy that is sustained no matter what. Being selfish is about two things: paying it forward and having faith.

So, stick around and get comfortable being uncomfortable. (You have been getting loads of practice at this so far in this book.) I invite you to identify that last piece of armour you may have up, that last dangling scrap of ego, and let it go. It's time to create a life of exponential meaning and connection.

If you dare.

## Reflection

· How do you define creativity?

· How do you express your creativity, either mentally or via more traditional art forms?

· Can you make a list of situations where you have solved or helped to solve a problem in a new and different way? How did you do it? How did it make you feel?

# CHALLENGE 8

# BE SELFLESS TO BE SELFISH

No-one is useless in this world who lightens the burdens of another.

– CHARLES DICKENS

234 UNREASONABLE AMBITION

I doubt there are many people in the Western world who haven't seen the British rom-com movie *Love Actually*. Whatever your views on the film, you'd be hard pressed to find someone who can't recall the opening scene in the arrival hall at Heathrow Airport.

We are greeted with successive moments of incoming passengers reuniting with their loved ones. What makes this scene so memorable is the emotion: the expressions on people's faces, the feelings we see in their eyes that are so palpable we can almost feel the love ourselves.

The scene reminds us that we are all connected, sometimes in unexpected ways; and that love is the one thing that binds us all together as human beings, irrespective of race, colour, creed or economics.

Love is the greatest unifier. You can't help but smile.

Here are the scene's opening lines, which are worth revisiting:

> *General opinion's starting to make out that we live in a world of hatred and greed, but I don't see that. It seems to me that love is everywhere.*

You might be guessing now what the final challenge might be? It's to switch the focus off yourself to others. To give back and pay it forward; even in those moments when you feel like you are depleted, dragging yourself along with nothing left in your tanks.

The rewards can be immeasurable.

# CHAPTER 29

# PAYING IT FORWARD

When we focus on others, our world expands.

– DANIEL GOLEMAN

Let's shake things up a little more and start with an uncomfortable declaration: *being selfless can be the best way to be selfish.* Research from optimism guru Martin Seligman shows that those who give are among the most successful people, and they live longer.

Don't believe me?

One of the most profound books I have ever read is called *Man's Search for Meaning.* It was written in 1946 by Viktor Frankl (an unreasonably ambitious leader; you met him in chapter 3). Frankl was a logotherapist who chronicled his experiences as an Auschwitz concentration camp survivor during World War II. When interviewed about how he endured and survived the experience, he described that he did so by focusing on someone other than himself. In his mind, he imagined the eventual reunion with his beloved wife. This fuelled his motivation and enabled him to stay hopeful even amid a seemingly hopeless situation. Frankl said:

> *My mind still clung to the image of my wife. A thought crossed my mind: I didn't even know if she were still alive. I knew only one thing, which I have learned well by now: love goes very far beyond the physical person of the beloved. Nothing could touch the strength of my love, and the thoughts of my beloved.*[84]

Frankl's story offers proof that everything can be taken away from us, except our ability to choose our mindset in any given circumstance. This is, as he said, 'the last of the human freedoms'.

But focusing on giving to others is not something we are instinctively pulled to do when we are feeling down, or find ourselves in the middle of one of life's many hurricanes. Giving to others in these situations almost feels unnatural, because we are hardwired for self-preservation – and yet it is *exactly what we need to do* to fill our cup to go another round.

This is also why asking for help can be so hard sometimes. The energy it takes to go towards people versus running away from them feels like an enormous effort. There may also exist a smattering of our ego wanting to keep up appearances for fear of judgement or of appearing less than we are.

I have noticed that unreasonably ambitious leaders rarely hesitate to go towards people in times of real need. They understand that getting help will enable them to nut through problems faster and get to resolution. But it takes humility and a fight against our natural instincts that tell us to either go into hibernation or go it alone.

In his standout TED Talk, *As Work Gets More Complex, 6 Rules to Simplify*, Boston Consulting Group legend Yves Morieux speaks to the need to foster cooperation if organisations want to maintain agility, speed and longevity in highly complex business environments.[85] He says the problem with how organisations are run is that they don't incentivise people to work together and help each other. Instead, he says, we create a 'middle office' or buy a 'second TV', which means people don't learn how to work together or negotiate important trade-offs.

According to Morieux, this is one of the biggest failings of current leadership practice. It creates environments in which the ego reigns and individualism is reinforced, to the detriment of productivity and overall effectiveness in the new world of work.

The final words of his TED Talk are formidable: 'Leaders should be punished for failing to cooperate and not fostering collaboration.'

Drop the mike.

## SOCIAL SUPPORT IS A TWO-WAY STREET

Morieux is bang on. Let's unpack the idea of leaders and their people exchanging support and look at the systemic impact on collective resilience.

**Social support increases our psychological willingness to drop our guard, lose the ego and cooperate.**

For years research into boosting mental toughness has touted the necessity of what we call 'social support' at work.[86] Social support helps us buffer negative experiences and boosts staying power towards outcomes that no one person can ever achieve on their own. Strong social support in an organisation is actually a precursor for fostering cooperation. It increases our psychological willingness to drop our guard, lose the ego and cooperate.

Social support can come in the form of receiving either psychological or material help from others, and giving it back. Just like any healthy and empowering dynamic it's a two-way street that's focused on a positive exchange.

Workplaces found to be stronger in social support tend to display significantly higher workplace outcomes such as increased commitment, job satisfaction and productivity. It's also a critical enabler for boosting people's moods during times of stress, giving them the strength to carry on and even flourish when tested.

You might be wondering why I am banging on so much about cooperation. I mean, what's so hard about it? I am talking about it because *it is not happening enough*. The act of exchanging support is not our natural default, particularly if we have been trained to work as lone wolves at work – usually because our rewards are tied to individual performance (I have come across many 'howlers').

Unreasonably ambitious leaders understand the opportunity that comes from working in a way that builds *intentional connection* with others. They see the larger-scale benefits this brings in realising their audacious goals.

Professional services firms provide a good example of where a shift in thinking around this would create significant impact. Having worked with many power brands at the top end of town over the years, I've witnessed hefty *cultural challenges* – usually linked to the behaviours of the organisations' high-performing technical leaders. These talented stars have usually achieved a cult-like status in their organisation because of their individual efforts. This makes the transition into a potential partner role a real test of character. From what I have observed, the biggest struggle is learning how to move their mindset from a self-serving 'I' so they can become an unreasonably ambitious leader focused on the greater 'we'. (I have witnessed some major crash-and-burns over the years!)

## SEEKING PEOPLE OUT AS YOUR DEFAULT

Unreasonably ambitious leaders usually work from a default position of seeking people out, rather than trying to avoid them. They spend most of their time focusing on building trust, making people awesome and fostering a strong sense of safety and belonging. It's why they often have 'paperless' desks; because they are rarely sitting at them! They're usually out and about, pressing the flesh (Raphaël Lapointe, who we met in chapter 5, was great at this!). These behaviours are the cornerstone to building *inclusive* and *collectively resilient* cultures.

I once worked with the executive team of a major electricity network provider. Many of the executives were struggling to get the pulse of their business and engage their 3000-strong workforce (not including contractors). I noticed a few things about how these executives engaged with their people:

- They were segregated on the tenth floor.
- They didn't go out and speak to people much (unless they needed something).
- Under stress, most of them went into a mental bunker and put a metaphorical 'you're not welcome' mat at their doorstep.
- They lived in their heads and solved problems alone.
- They didn't really know their people.

So, what was different about the one executive who stood out from the rest? He was someone I immediately identified as a counter-cultural hire. He:

- set up a hot-desk arrangement where each week he worked from a different floor
- conducted regular 'listening tours' on the ground, asking lots of questions and engaging his people in collaborative problem-solving
- knew his people personally, and got together with them informally and regularly (he was the only executive who knew most people's names)

- was vulnerable and shared his trials and tribulations (he lost his leg and suffered burns to 50% of his body in the 2002 Bali bombings)
- was the executive member people approached most; people greeted him on the floor and in the lift with beaming smiles.

You may be wondering what happened to him? Did he stay on to become the next CEO?

He moved on to become the CEO of a big player energy retailer. Unreasonably ambitious as always, he is looking to disrupt his organisation and transform his sector. A couple of his quotable quotes that have stuck with me over the years include:

- 'Grab adversity and look it in the eyes. Don't waste your energy on things you can't control.' This is how he survived his injuries from the bombings (but that is a whole other book).
- 'People are everything. Focus on them.' Building relationships, asking for and accepting help and actively keeping his network alive is where he spends most of his time.

## HOW ABOUT YOU?

Christmas is often a tough time for people. If you're feeling blue, instead of focusing on what you don't have, spend the day helping serve Christmas dinner to the homeless. It's the fastest way to snap yourself out of a funk and get back to making your dent in the universe.

Let me explain how it works on your psyche. Taking the focus off yourself provides your mind with a welcome break from melancholy and related stress. The emotions that are generated from giving ignite an immediate change in perspective. The resulting feelings will likely ground you and spark gratitude for what you *do have* – what is going well in your life – and take your focus off what's missing.

Take a moment to think about leaders you have met during your life that are unreasonably ambitious. You will recall how lively and positive they tend to be. How generous they often are. How intoxicating their energy is. Which makes perfect sense. Positive psychology research demonstrates that those who experience feelings of gratitude more often are happier people, and are more likely to relish experiences and deal better with adversity.

So how are you feeling right now? I hope I have convinced you not to give in to the usual wallowing, but to try a different approach.

But once you're there how do you stay there? How do you maintain your positive edge? I have saved the best until last. In chapter 30 we are going to talk about spirituality and purposeful energy. It's a taboo zone we don't usually discuss in the hard-arse world of business.

But learning how to *lead with soul* is next-level evolution. It's what sustains you when the lights go out.

**Learning how to lead with soul is next-level evolution.**

Take a deep breath, and let's dive under the waves.

## Reflection

- What's something you could try to elevate your state of mind within seconds?

- What could you do to boost your gratitude for life in an instant?

# CHAPTER 30

# GOD HAS LEFT THE BUILDING

The world is full of magic things, patiently waiting for our senses to grow sharper.

– WB YEATS

We live in a world divided.

For centuries our history has been defined by gargantuan acts of human bravery that have changed the course of life as we know it. Most of these were fuelled by divergent beliefs and faith in a sentient being, steering us in a direction of a higher power and yet bestowing upon us the free will to make decisions that align with that value system.

It's ironic that religion and related notions of spirituality have also been primary catalysts for many a war and other atrocities, resulting in the destruction and annihilation of countless civilisations, countries and human lives. It's an unparalleled source of human conflict and suffering.

It's where we have become divided; why humanity has lost faith and been set adrift from what matters most; why it feels like we've lost our way.

We've gone back to revering false idols and chasing a hedonistic lifestyle that would make Roman Emperor Caligula proud. And we're paying the price, with chronic mental health issues and people reportedly languishing, looking at their life through a foggy windscreen.

A fascinating pan-European study by Stephen Bullivant, Professor of Theology at St Mary's University, London, showed that in a dozen countries we have become 'irreligious' as a society.[87]

*God has indeed left the building.*

With so many losing faith in God and what traditional religion has to offer, it's worthwhile wondering: what is filling the space that has been vacated, and what does that mean for our lives and work? Even if you've never been a churchgoer, you may know the purpose of church has always been more than simply unifying people around a shared religion. It has also been a gathering place for the like-minded to grow community and connect more deeply around a rallying belief. It has been a lifeline for tormented souls to stay afloat; for people to love and be loved.

Groundbreaking research into the role faith plays in boosting positive mental health outcomes is also well-documented. Actively nurturing our spiritual development brings immeasurable benefits.[88]

So where does this leave us? Things have changed and the onus to make decisions about what our existence should be, to chart the course to a meaningful life, to shape our destinies – is now on us. And it's causing major existential upheaval.

Life feels more precarious than it has ever been. Most people feel like they have even less control over their lives than ever. At work, it has become common to see leaders replace faith with cynicism, integrity with loose morals, respect for others with mistreatment and neglect and compassion with abuse.

So, what do we do about it? How do unreasonably ambitious leaders maintain their moral compass and stay on track when things have become so murky? Where do they find the energy to wade through times of crisis and not burn out? Without the anchor of an institution, how do they maintain their belief in a higher purpose and keep their faith in a brighter future?

## Reflection

- How do you keep the faith and stay buoyant during tough times?

- How do you make decisions about what is right and what is wrong?

- What are some of the practices you engage in to cultivate your own spirituality?

## REDEFINING SPIRITUALITY FOR MODERN TIMES

Whether you believe in God, Buddha or something else entirely, it's up to you to define spirituality in a way that works for you. It starts with knowing exactly what it is that nourishes your soul when it you need it the most.

For the purposes of our work together, I define spirituality as *the power derived from having a sense of purpose in your life and a connectedness to something greater*. It is the alignment between what you say is important in your life and the way you live. It is your belief in what is possible, and that there is a reason for your being that is bigger than you. The stronger the alignment, the more powerful your spirituality will be as a source of energy and renewal in every part of your life.

> **Spirituality is the power derived from having a sense of purpose in your life and a connectedness to something greater.**

## SPIRITUALITY AT WORK

A focus on sheer brain power is insufficient to drive peak performance outcomes under pressure at work. This is well evidenced in the literature. And guess what garners the top spot in jump-starting peak performance under pressure? Spirituality.

In their acclaimed research into what makes a 'corporate athlete', Jim Loehr and Tony Schwartz found that the ideal performance state happens when all parts of ourselves – body, mind and spirit – are working together holistically.[89]

The magic happens when your physical energy, emotional calm and mental focus are powered by your deepest values; by your connection to a higher purpose.

If this is sounding a bit like a foreign language, think of your guiding purpose as a human battery pack. It's how you sustain yourself and keep shining your light on the world.

> **Think of your guiding purpose as a human battery pack.**

Unreasonably ambitious leaders can maintain their high performance – even in the face of repetitive knockbacks, harsh conditions and berating – by concentrating their energy in the service of realising their purpose (think about the entrepreneur's journey we talked about in chapter 8). It enables them to hang in there during the rollercoaster ride of doing business today.

Look at the high-performance pyramid in the figure below. The model illustrates the relationships between our different parts of self, and how they all work together. It's a useful tool to audit where you are investing your energy and where you need to reload your stores.[90]

High Performance Pyramid

RITUALS
RITUALS
SPIRITUAL CAPACITY
Provides a powerful source of motivation, determination and endurance
MENTAL CAPACITY
Focuses physical and emotional energy on the task at hand
RITUALS
RITUALS
EMOTIONAL CAPACITY
Creates the internal climate that drives the ideal performance state
PHYSICAL CAPACITY
Builds endurance and promotes mental and emotional recovery
RITUALS

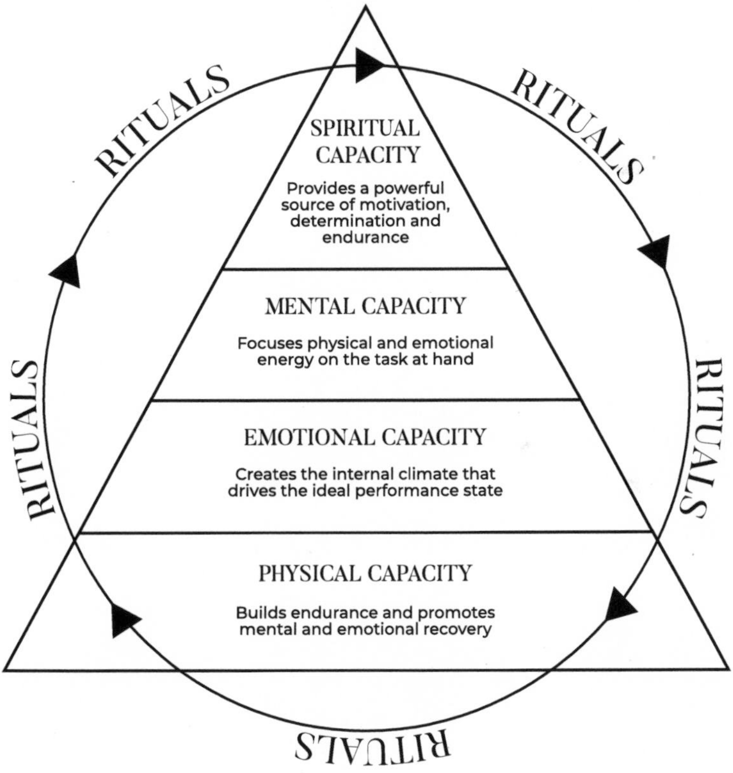

Source: Loehr, J and Schwartz, T (2001), 'The Making of a Corporate Athlete', *Harvard Business Review*, hbr.org/2001/01/the-making-of-a-corporate-athlete.

And nurturing your spiritual capacity is the cherry on the sundae. It's the 'energiser bunny' for sustained resilience and maximising your impact, particularly when the going gets tough. Whether they formally deem themselves spiritual or not, unreasonably ambitious leaders are always tapped into a deeper sense of who they are, what they stand for and what the world needs from them.

## A PURPOSE-DRIVEN LIFE

Leading a purpose-driven life serves as extra sustenance in the face of adversity, and is a powerful source of motivation and focus. On the flip side, knowing what you value and what drives you can also be a huge source of angst and dissatisfaction, particularly if you are not living a life true to them. This can cause disengagement and seriously affect your staying power. It's why I always start my work with clients here: with the end in mind.

To illustrate, let me share Gaston's story with you. Gaston was the CFO of a large federal government-run department responsible for curating Canada's cultural heritage sites, artworks and national treasures. He was being considered for a promotion into a director-general role. He was highly regarded, well-liked and considered a shoo-in for the position. He'd been with the department for aeons.

I must admit, I wasn't all that excited to meet Gaston. Stuffy finance guys weren't always that engaging, and I expected that Gaston would have become robotic and institutionalised after years of service in the public sector.

When Gaston walked into my office, I smiled knowingly to myself. He was short in stature and had hair that looked like it had been stuck down with Brylcreem. His look was dorky but endearing. What really stood out was his outfit. He was wearing a standard navy-blue suit and, wait for it, holding an Akubra in his hand. It was totally out of place, and it threw me.

*This could get interesting*, I thought to myself.

As we started the meeting, his energy was flat; his responses to my questions lacklustre. I wondered why they sent him to me for testing, and thought maybe they were just ticking a box after all his years of service. I mean, watching a kettle boil was more exciting than having a conversation with him!

And then it hit me. This was not his fault. It was mine. It was on me to find a way to connect with him. I realised in that moment I was so blinded by my own biases that I hadn't really given him a chance. (Don't judge me too harshly; psychologists are human too!)

And then, out of nowhere, a question came into my mind.

'Gaston, I'd like to ask you a bit of an unusual question.' I was a little nervous asking him, but I had nothing to lose at this point. I had to try something different.

'*Mais oui,*' he replied gently.

'What did you want to be when you were a child? What did you imagine you would be doing when you grew up?'

My words hung in the air. I have no idea why I asked him that. It was one of my inexplicable intuitive moments.

His face glowed. I sensed I was onto something.

'Elvis,' he said bashfully.

'*Elvis?*'

'*Oui*, Elvis.' He smiled.

'Right. Well, let's talk about that. Can you sing?' (I wanted to explore whether this was a viable career path.)

'Of course I can sing,' he replied.

'Okay, hit me with your best rendition of 'Blue Suede Shoes', right here, right now.' I was laughing at this point. I mean, how good could this guy really be? Give me a break!

Gaston stood up, turned his back to me and then swung back around quickly, wearing the Elvis snarl face. He sang 'Blue Suede Shoes'. And he was amazing! I was not prepared for this at all.

Watching a client transform like that right before my eyes was magic in action.

When Gaston entered my office, he was miserable; going through the motions on a path he felt he needed to pursue – not one that stirred his soul. He had traded his passion for obligation.

But by tapping into his purpose, he found renewed energy for his work and life. *Happiness should never be a trade-off.*

You'll be happy to know Gaston ended up leaving his organisation and landed regular gigs as an Elvis impersonator. I don't know if he ever went back to his day job.

## RITUALS FOR RENEWAL

Living a life of purpose means directing your energy to:

· something you love doing
· something the world needs
· something that pays you well
· something you are good at.

Unreasonably ambitious leaders are prepared to ask themselves the hard questions, do the work to figure out their bigger why, and then execute on their passion. Back in part II we explored values and how to connect to a deeper purpose or reason for being. To take this next level we have to move spirituality into action by practising *rituals*.

Rituals are defined as 'a patterned, repetitive and symbolic enactment of a cultural belief or value'.[91] Developing rituals specifically to nourish your spiritual side will enable you to reap the benefits of a renewed focus.

A physical ritual might be following a daily gym routine. An emotional ritual might be going to a counsellor once a month. A mental ritual might be writing down all your tasks you didn't complete to declutter your mind before going to bed.

On the spiritual front, I like to think of rituals as *modern-day acts of faith*, dedicated to putting your purpose into practice every day to keep you on track.

Whichever way you slice it, rituals promote more conscious habits and choices. They not only mark time, but they also create time. They bring to your consciousness the things you need to say no to, to create space for the things you want to say yes to.

If you're wondering where to start with your rituals, there are lots you could put into practice. The ones I like best are:

· meditation
· mindfulness
· journalling
· practising gratitude
· being of service to others
· prayer
· creative visualisation.

I like to think of rituals as modern-day acts of faith.

## Reflection

- Which rituals could you realistically incorporate into your daily routines? If they are too 'out there' or they don't feel right, you probably won't last the distance long term.

- Can you come up with a ritual for each area of the pyramid – physical, emotional, mental and spiritual?

- What bad habits or practices do you currently engage in that are not serving you, that sap your energy, that you could shed?

## UNREASONABLY AMBITIOUS ENERGY

If you're feeling like you're up for an even bigger challenge and you are ready for an energy overhaul, I have a three-step process for you to work through, which ends with the development of your rituals. I recommend taking some time out from the rat race to do this work if you can. Unreasonably ambitious leaders tend to take time out once or twice a year to get away and work on becoming aligned and centred. It assists them in refocusing their energy where it matters most, and revitalises their commitment to their goals and purpose.

It begins with figuring out how you are currently managing your own energy using a simple and powerful medicine wheel activity. Have you heard of medicine wheels before? If you haven't, you're in for a treat. Medicine wheels have been used for centuries and are found in many different cultures. They depict all that is good and life-giving. The four quadrants of a medicine wheel, pictured in the figure below, represent a perfect balance or the circle of life. The wheel depicts the balance between mind, body, spirit and emotion.

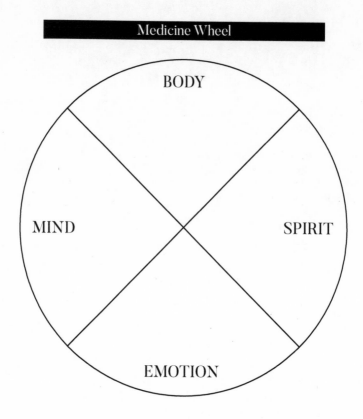

Medicine Wheel

BODY

MIND

SPIRIT

EMOTION

Spiritual development and self-development occur when you attend to and challenge yourself in each area.

Here's how it's done.

## Step 1

Use the medicine wheel to guide your thinking about the various activities you currently engage in. In each quadrant, write keywords or draw pictures to depict what you are currently doing to feed, express and extend that aspect of yourself.

Where do you have less of a focus? Where do you over-focus? Out of a total score of 100 assign the percentage of time you spend in each area of the wheel.

Think about how you might redistribute the energy in the quadrants by developing rituals for each part of the wheel to create balance across all parts of you.

## Step 2

Visualisation is a wonderful tool you can use when you are feeling out of alignment with your values and need to reconnect to your core purpose.

Close your eyes and picture something or someone who inspires you.

Sit with this feeling as you take a few very deep breaths.

What images came to your mind?

How do these images inspire you to act today?

Imagine yourself radiating this image today.

What will you say, think and do?

## Step 3

Build rituals to reinforce your priorities and sustain your energy, so you can focus on what matters most.

\*

How are you feeling right now? I hope you feel refreshed and sparked with renewed optimism and blazing motivation to start flexing your mindset muscles.

I've been very clear about what is required to kit out your mind and awaken the sleeping giant within you. You are well on the road to realising your own unreasonable ambitions.

To finish up our adventure together, let's take stock of all we have learned. Part IV, momentum, brings together the highlights of our journey. It's my last-ditch effort to make sure you were listening and to show my commitment to supporting your unparalleled success and long-term happiness.

So, stick with me as we wrap up all our learnings with a technicolour bow.

## Reflection

- What epiphany did you have about where your attention, focus and energy is going?

- Identify your biggest life and work challenges right now. Is there a link between these and where your energy management is most depleted?

- What can you do to distribute your energy and attention more evenly?

# PART IV
# MOMEN TUM

We do not need magic to change the world, we carry all the power we need inside ourselves already: we have the power to imagine better.

– JK ROWLING

Thanks for staying with me.

My goal in writing this book was to create curiosity and enlightenment. The information in its pages is intended to be life-changing.

Here are the questions I set out to answer for my readers:

- How can I best use the gifts and talents I have for the purpose of making those around me, and the world, better?
- How can I create a life that exceeds my expectations beyond measure?
- How can I lead a life of unreasonable ambition?

I've been upfront with you about the audacious journey that lies ahead of you, irrespective of how far along you are already or how far you still have to go. After reading this book, I'm hoping I've convinced you of what you have known all along – that you're itching to proudly wear the suit of the unreasonably ambitious leader. That you're ready to fully tap into your bravery and quest for adventure as an explorer. That you're primed to be a pioneer leading yourself and others to the edge of new frontiers – while also accepting that this may mean you sometimes stand alone.

I hope you now know that the force inside you is compelling you to act. And that in the end, it will all be worth it.

## YOU'RE A NATURAL BORN RENEGADE

If you made it to the end of this book, I will assume that you felt a connection with the renegade thinking presented to you and that you have accepted the challenge I set for you – to do the work to be the best version of yourself.

I believe in you and I know you can do this, just like I have. Deep inside, you know that your unreasonably ambitious soul has always been part of who you are. Perhaps this book has given you the nudge you need to fully own it with strength and conviction – knowing that you are not alone in your quest.

There is no set time for stepping up to the calling. Your clock will tick at the right speed for you, when you are ready. Place your trust in that. Be reassured that you are exactly where you are meant to be right now in this moment – just as you are.

## TRUST THAT IT WILL COME

My own realisation around thinking differently started when I was a child. I remember it vividly. When I was about 11, I would ride my bike to the local library and spend Saturdays curled up on a beanbag, devouring any books I could get my hands on about folklore, mythology and ancient yarns from around the world. Wrapping my mind up in tales of adventure, magic and the impossible created a protective shield against the reality of a broken home, and the darkness that hovered over me as I dealt with the demons that attacked my peace.

During those formative years, my love of literature was a blessing. It was hard to form relationships with other children my age. Instead, books were my reliable friends and provided me with the comfort and space to escape. Getting lost in their pages boosted my resilience, evolved my mind, and helped me form a resolute moral compass to navigate the swings and roundabouts of my developing life. (Monseigneur Bienvenu, the bishop in Victor Hugo's 1862 novel *Les Misérables*, is a role model for me in terms of the compassion and forgiveness he extended to the thief Jean Valjean.)

When I finally looked up from the pages as an adult, I realised something pivotal. Life is not a fairy tale (although many moments of magic exist); *it is what we make of it that counts.*

Interestingly, out of all the stories I have read over my lifetime, I have learned some of the more powerful lessons from Chinese mythology. Unlike the more well-known Greek and Roman myths, the Chinese believe that becoming a 'deity' is not reserved for some magical omnipotent being but is a right bestowed on any mortals who have done extraordinary deeds and left a legacy.

I believe that we are all born renegades with unreasonable ambition. The difference between myself and others – in that I recognised this earlier than most – can be attributed to the fact that *life circumstances forced me to access my gifts sooner.*

Much like many of the leaders we have met in these pages, it was the tough conditions of my childhood that played a forcing function in my own evolution to make intentional choices about how to live my life. It became a matter of survival.

My success happened when I became fully cognisant of my own gifts, and learned how to access them and then leverage them in the pursuit of higher-order goals.

*To get real momentum you must understand that living a life of unreasonable ambition is a mindset; and success is a conscious choice.*

## MAKING IT HAPPEN

To gather this momentum you need to awaken your sleeping giant. In this book I have presented you with eight adaptive challenges to take control of your mind and lead your life and work in your desired direction.

But interest, information and access are not enough if you don't do anything with them. You are in control of what happens next. A *maniacal focus on action* is what makes the difference between a genius who flips burgers for a living and an average leader who becomes a billionaire. If you don't use it, you lose it!

Let's do a quick recap on what you've learned:

- You've learned to welcome stress and capitalise on energy to activate your impact.
- You're ready to embrace the healing properties of pain and emotions as essential ingredients to your ongoing evolution.
- You understand how to get control of your emotions and step into life with mental toughness and grit.
- You've built your skills to see into the future – tapping into your intuition to be on the front foot about what's to come, so you can get excited by it.
- You've unlocked your creative side and expanded your mindset to see a limitless view.
- You're confident in stepping into the unknown and know how to supercharge your productivity to get results even in the eye of the storm.

- You have made fun a priority in your life and maintain a fresh perspective while keeping the faith.
- You know that giving back to others is the most powerful way to move your mind into an enhanced state of being.
- You've realised the absolute profound impact your mind has on performance and life fulfilment.
- You know that your success and happiness is in your hands.

## WHAT'S NEXT?

Our lives are going to change dramatically over the next five to ten years, influenced by the people we meet and the books we read.

My commitment to you is:

- that I am here for you
- that I will create a community for you to get the support you need to uphold an unreasonably ambitious life
- that I will continue to write and speak and share my renegade thinking in the hope that you will always find value and comfort in the space I hold for you – knowing you are not alone, and you can always find me.

I've already started putting pen to paper for the next development of this book, giving you the tools and inspiration to create unreasonable ambition at scale with your people and organisations, and achieve impossible change – because *sustaining success is a team sport, not a solo act.*

The onus is now on you to be a catalyst for impossible change. To create the life you were born to live. To be the renegade leader you have always been.

Now that you see, there's no turning back.

Being unreasonably ambitious means you have chosen to be a city on a hill – elevated, bold and visible, a beacon of light for the world to see and others to follow.

Now go be it!

# ACKNOWLEDGEMENTS

Writing *Unreasonable Ambition* has been an incredible creative journey resulting in deep gratitude. I acknowledge all of those still with me, and those who have passed, who have contributed to this book – if not in person, in spirit.

I have had many guardian angels enter my life at different moments when I needed them the most. They've dusted off my wings and helped me to fly, so that I might give voice to my soul's rumblings, my heart's loudest whispers, and share them with the world.

To my grandmother Lia and grandfather Marius who led an unreasonably ambitious trail-blazing life and have provided me with unparalleled inspiration.

To my parents Penelope and Robert who found their true north and evolved into conscious and compassionate human beings.

To my devoted husband Jason for providing me with unconditional love and the space to create my life's work in this book and beyond.

To my children Noah and Allegra for filling my heart with joy and helping me see the world through eyes of wonder every day.

To my little tribe of true friends for their unwavering support and for lifting me up in my darkest moments.

To my teacher, Dr Peter Sevastos, thank you for blowing up the obstacles on my road to a career trajectory I could never have imagined, and for believing in me when I didn't believe in myself.

To my support crew of amazing colleagues and clients who continue to back me, place their trust in me and allow me to guide them in living their best lives.

To the leaders in this book, for sharing your most sacred moments with me and for the sacrifice and commitments you make to creating a better world.

To God, our creator, for giving me the faith to keep going against the odds.

# WHO IS VANESSA VERSHAW?

*VANESSA VERSHAW HAS RELENTLESS BELIEF IN HUMAN POTENTIAL*

Recognised as an elite peak-performance coaching psychologist, entrepreneur and transformation strategist, she is a trusted advisor to executives, key decision-makers, ASX-20 and Fortune 100 organisations globally.

Vanessa has dedicated over two decades to helping leaders reimagine their futures using a potent combination of business psychology, design thinking, neuroscience and ancient wisdom. A visionary born with a fire raging within, she empowers leaders to shift their mindsets towards resilience, adaptability and big-hearted ambition.

A former budding Journalist with the ABC, her media features include Channel 7, 10 as well as regular appearance on Channel 9 as a Workplace Psychologist. Vanessa is also a regular on national radio covering topics around future of work, diversity, inclusion, leadership, organisational psychology, transformation, and world issues. She has been published and featured in The Australian, Financial Review; Diplomat Magazine, The Globe and Mail, The Ottawa Citizen, Ottawa Business Journal, WA Business News and Emergent Magazine to name but a few.

Her most significant achievement is as a proud mother of two. Vanessa loves to travel, cross-country ski, box, run and write. She's inspired by the arts, random acts of kindness, and people whose souls are impatient to evolve.

# NEED MORE OF VANESSA IN YOUR LIFE?

Want some more Vanessa Vershaw in your life?

If this book has been a gamechanger for you, there are a number of ways you can work with Vanessa. Check out the information on her website vanessavershaw.com and follow her on Linkedin, Instagram, and Facebook.

# WHO DO YOU KNOW THAT NEEDS THIS BOOK?

Who do you know that needs this book in their life?

The perfect gift for clients, teams and colleagues - gift Unreasonable Ambition to the leaders and big thinkers in your world.

Reach out to hello@vanessavershaw.com to discuss the options for bulk orders and personalised gifts for your upcoming events.

# SPEAKING

*"Engaging, insightful, mesmerising, fascinating, challenging, intoxicating, captivating."*

Need a dynamic, highly experienced world class speaker for your next live or virtual event?

Vanessa is frequently sought out to motivate, inspire and deliver though leadership to some of the most respected companies in the world.

Vanessa is a renowned authority on the following topics;

Leading through chaos and change
Renegade thinking for a brave new world
When resilience is not enough
Accelerating human potential
Becoming purpose-led
Entrepreneurship and innovation
DEI and social impact

Contact Vanessa to discuss your next event and options for keynotes, facilitation, panel discussions, interviewing and presentations.

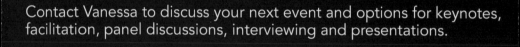

# INTERVIEW VANESSA

A former budding Journalist with the ABC, her media features include Channel 7, 10 as well as regula appearance on Channel 9 as a Workplace Psychologist Vanessa is also a regular on national radio covering topics around future of work, diversity, inclusion, leadership business psychology, transformation, and world issues. She has been published and featured in The Australian Financial Review; Diplomat Magazine, The Globe and Mail The Ottawa Citizen, Ottawa Business Journal, WA Business News and Emergent Magazine to name but a few

If you would like to interview Vanessa about her latest book, Unreasonable Ambition, or any of the topics above please email hello@vanessavershaw.com. Vanessa also loves participating as part of a panel

VANESSA VERSHAW RUNS A GLOBAL ADVISORY SPECIALISING IN LEADERSHIP, CULTURE AND STRATEGY

*"Leave a legacy you're proud of.'*

# EXECUTIVE COACHING & DEVELOPMENT

## NOT ALL COACHES ARE CREATED EQUAL

Vanessa is focussed on powering up leaders and teams to realise their personal and workplace ambitions and accelerating the possible.

Amplifying potential equates to experimenting with brave new approaches to shift outdated ways of thinking and operating.

Coaching with Vanessa will prepare leaders and teams to confidently tackle the future as renegade thinkers and radical problem-solvers.

Draw from her vast expertise with ASX-20 and Fortune 100 companies in high performance coaching, psychology, neuroscience, and personal transformation. Vanessa helps break-through the limits of current thinking to achieve both sustained exponential growth and mastery.

Vanessa works with a select number of individuals and teams each year, to find out more about working with her, please email hello@vanessavershaw.com.

# STRATEGY & CULTURE

## THINK ABOUT YOUR MOST FAVOURITE WORKPLACE

Culture journeys involve time, faith, bravery and commitment to leaving a legacy. Aligned with forward-looking strategy, growth-oriented and adaptive leaders, culture is your strongest driver of competitive advantage.

Vanessa's work with organisations and leaders involves interweaving psychological dexterity into the fabric of culture and building creative strategies to future proof business performance and rapidly flex to ongoing disruption.

With a proven history of assisting organisations to take control and cultivate adaptive, people-centred cultures and strategy that drive real business results - Vanessa does this by:

- Doing strategy differently – using creative techniques and rigorous methodology to derive award winning strategies to future-proof and evolve organisations.
- Building leadership bench strength – advising on top team and board effectiveness plays for optimised performance outcomes.
- Designing workplace well-being and health strategies to boost collective resilience.
- Creating powerful purpose-led organisational initiatives.
- Evaluating and implementing adaptive culture change methodologies to design growth-oriented culture strategies.
- Unlocking limitless potential for creativity and innovation with leaders and teams.
- Building bolder, conscious leaders with the skills to lead into the future with confidence and courage at scale.

Talk to us about how to navigate the unknown with confidence.

# ENDNOTES

1  Adams, T (2022), 'Mining Industry's economic contribution to Australia', Global Road Technology, globalroadtechnology.com/mining-industrys-economic-contribution-to-australia.

2  Seale, A (2016), 'The Liminal Space – Embracing the Mystery and Power of Transition from What Has Been to What Will Be', Center for Transformational Presence, transformationalpresence.org/alan-seale-blog/liminal-space-embracing-mystery-power-transition-will-2.

3  A 'black swan' event is a low-probability, unpredictable and unforeseen event, typically one with extreme consequences. A 'grey rhino' event is a slowly emerging, obvious threat that is ignored or minimised by decision-makers. The climate crisis and disruptive technologies are two examples of this type of threat. Grey rhinos are also called 'known unknowns'.

4  Heifetz, RA, Linsky, M and Grashow, A (2009), *The Practice of Adaptive Leadership: Tools and Tactics for Changing Your Organization and the World*, Harvard Business Review Press.

5  Mitchell, A (2017), 'CIO: The 6 c's of success for c-suite execs', Bendelta, bendelta.com/cio-the-6-cs-of-success-for-c-suite-execs.

6  Grant, A (2016), *Originals: How Non-Conformists Move the World*, WH Allen.

7  The Fourth Industrial Revolution is the ongoing automation of traditional manufacturing and industrial practices, using modern smart technology.

8  Mitchell, A (2017), op. cit.

9  Forgive me for this quote not being respectful of all genders. Thankfully we have come a long way since then.

10 Moses is considered one of the most important prophets in Judaism who holds out his staff for God to part the waters of the Red Sea to help the Israelite slaves escape the pursuing Egyptians (as recounted in the Book of Exodus).

11 'Ranga' is an abbreviation of 'orangutan'. Used mostly in Australia, the word has gradually spread across the world and has now been adopted to refer to all redheads, usually in a derogatory manner.

12 Denning, S (2015), 'Learning Consortium For The Creative Economy', *Forbes*, forbes.com/sites/stevedenning/2015/11/02/ drucker-forum-2015-tackles-the-creative-economy/ ?sh=3af265781697.

13 The Desjardins Group is a Canadian financial services cooperative and the largest federation of credit unions in North America. It was founded in 1900 in Lévis, Quebec by Alphonse Desjardins. While its legal headquarters remains in Lévis, most of the executive management, including the CEO, is based in Montréal.

14 Henry Higgins is a fictional character – a professor of phonetics who makes a bet that he can teach Cockney flower girl Eliza Doolittle how to speak proper English, in George Bernard Shaw's play *Pygmalion* (1913).

15 Bringmann, HC et al. (2021), 'Mantra meditation as adjunctive therapy in major depression: A randomized controlled trial', *Journal of Affective Disorders* (6), 100232.

16 Snyder, M (1986), *Public Appearances, Private Realities: The Psychology of Self-Monitoring*, WH Freeman & Company.

17 Eurich, T (2018), *Insight: The Surprising Truth About How Others See Us, How We See Ourselves, and Why the Answers Matter More Than We Think*, Currency.

18 Sinek, S (2017), *Leaders Eat Last: Why Some Teams Pull Together and Others Don't*, Portfolio.

19 Kiyosaki, R and Lechter, S (1997), *Rich Dad Poor Dad*, Plata Publishing.

20 Hesselbein, F, Goldsmith, M and Beckhard, R (eds.; 1997), *The Leader of the Future*, Jossey-Bass.

21 Furr, N and Furr, SH (2022), *The Upside of Uncertainty: A Guide to Finding Possibility in the Unknown*, Harvard Business Review Press.

22 Ibid.

23 Carse, J (2013), *Finite and Infinite Games: A Vision of Life as Play and Possibility*, Free Press.

24 Kotler, S and Wheal, J (2017), *Stealing Fire: How Silicon Valley, the Navy SEALs, and Maverick Scientists are Revolutionizing the Way We Live and Work*, HarperCollins US.

25 World Health Organization (2019), 'Burn-out an "occupational phenomenon": International Classification of Diseases', who.int/news/item/28-05-2019-burn-out-an-occupational-phenomenon-international-classification-of-diseases.

26 Salt, B (2016), 'Moralisers, we need you!', *The Australian*, theaustralian.com.au/weekend-australian-magazine/moralisers-we-need-you/news-story/6bdb24f77572be68330bd306c14ee8a3.

27 Neubauer, R, Tarling, A and Wade, M (2017), *Redefining leadership for a Digital Age*, IMD Publications.

28 Ventura, M (2018), *Applied Empathy: The New Language of Leadership*, Atria Books.

29 Malik, O (2016), 'Silicon Valley has an empathy vacuum', *The New Yorker*, newyorker.com/business/currency/silicon-valley-has-an-empathy-vacuum.

30 Ignatius, A (2021), 'Microsoft's Satya Nadella on Flexible Work, the Metaverse, and the Power of Empathy', *Harvard Business Review*, hbr.org/2021/10/microsofts-satya-nadella-on-flexible-work-the-metaverse-and-the-power-of-empathy.

31 Gonzales, L (2004), *Deep Survival: Who Lives, Who Dies, and Why*, WW Norton & Company.

32 David, S (2016), *Emotional Agility: Get Unstuck, Embrace Change and Thrive in Work and Life*, Avery Publishing Group.

33 Western Power is a Western Australian State Government-owned corporation delivering a safe, reliable and affordable energy supply to 2.3 million people.

34 AEMO manages electricity and gas systems and markets across Australia.

35 The so-called 'spidey sense' or 'spider sense' generally refers to an extraordinary ability to sense imminent danger, a kind of 'sixth sense' attributed to the comic-book superhero Spider-Man.

36 *The Economist* (2012), 'The last Kodak moment?', economist.com/business/2012/01/14/the-last-kodak-moment.

37 Duke, A (2022), *Quit: The Power of Knowing When to Walk Away*, Portfolio Books.

38 Petski, D (2021), 'Stratagem Stages Launch with Paramount Series, Stratagem, stratagemgroup.ca/2021/05/25/stratagem-stages-launch-with-paramount-series.

39 Halligan, B (2019), 'Can small companies pull off an Uber?', Medium, medium.com/@HubSpot/can-small-companies-pull-off-an-uber-1863c9c2e4.

40 Wade, M, Tarling, A and Neubauer, R (2017), *Redefining Leadership for a Digital Age*, IMD, imd.org/research-knowledge/reports/redefining-leadership.

41 Ibid.

42 O'Brien, PD (2019), *Intuitive Intelligence: Make Life-Changing Decisions with Perfect Timing*, Beyond Words Publishing.

43 Young, G (2011), 'The Multiple Parts of the Self', *Psychology Today*, psychologytoday.com/us/blog/rejoining-joy/201103/the-multiple-parts-the-self.

44 Kotler, S (2021), *The Art of Impossible: A Peak Performance Primer*, HarperCollins.

45 Epstein, D (2021), *Range: Why Generalists Triumph in a Specialized World*, Pan Macmillan.

46 Morgan, B (2021), 'Who Wins The Battle Of Walmart Vs. Amazon?', *Forbes*, forbes.com/sites/blakemorgan/2021/06/14/who-wins-the-battle-of-walmart-vs-amazon/?sh=2fc1b3695ba7.

47 Goldsmith, M (2007), *What Got You Here Won't Get You There: How Successful People Become Even More Successful*, Hyperion.

48 Karpinski, RI et al. (2018), 'High intelligence: A risk factor for psychological and physiological overexcitabilities', *Intelligence*, vol. 66, pp. 8–23.

49 Liberman, B (host) and Beth Gibson (producer) (17 October 2017), 'Jostein Solheim: CEO, Futurist, All Round Champ', *Dumbo Feather Podcast*.

50 Grant, A (2016), *Originals: How Non-Conformists Change the World*, Penguin Random House.

51  Eliot, TS (1925), 'The Hollow Men'.

52  Gage, D (2012), 'The Venture Capital Secret: 3 Out of 4 Start-Ups Fail', *The Wall Street Journal*, wsj.com/articles/SB100008723963904 43720204578004980476429190.

53  Rose-Clance, P and Imes, S (1978), 'The Imposter Phenomenon in High Achieving Women: Dynamics and Therapeutic Intervention', *Psychotherapy Theory, Research and Practice*, vol. 15, no. 3.

54  Murali, M (2020), '"You Have to Believe in Yourself When No One Else Does" – Serena Williams Addresses Class of 2020 at Mouratoglou's Academy', Essentially Sports, essentiallysports.com/ tennis-news-wta-you-have-to-believe-in-yourself-when-no-one-else-does-serena-williams-addresses-class-of-2020-at-mouratoglous-academy.

55  Sonstroem, E (2010), 'Why Do Mexican Jumping Beans Jump?', A Moment of Science, https://indianapublicmedia.org/ amomentofscience/mexican-jumping-beans-jump.php.

56  Sieden, LS (2012), *A Fuller View: Buckminster Fuller's Vision of Hope and Abundance for All*, Divine Arts.

57  Dweck, CS (2007), *Mindset: The New Psychology of Success*, Ballantine Books.

58  Ramsay, TZ and Skov, M (2010), 'How Genes Make Up Your Mind: Individual Biological Differences and Values-based Decisions', *Journal of Economic Psychology*, vol. 31, no. 5, pp. 818–831.

59  Furr, N and Furr, SH (2022), *The Upside of Uncertainty: A Guide to Finding Possibility in the Unknown*, Harvard Business Review Press.

60  Taleb, NN (2012), *Antifragile: Things that Gain from Disorder*, Penguin Books.

61  Reeves, M, O'Dea, A and Carlsson-Szlezack, P (2022), 'Make resilience your company's strategic advantage', *Harvard Business Review*, hbr.org/2022/03/make-resilience-your-companys-strategic-advantage.

62  Schnieder, Dr G and Mcguirk, T (2022), 'The move towards Presilience', IFSEC Global, ifsecglobal.com/security/the-move-towards-presilience.

63 Schneider, G (n.d.), 'Why a Presilience mindset is crucial for thriving in the new normal', Business Daily Media, businessdailymedia.com/sme-business-news/4810-why-a-presilience-mindset-is-crucial-for-thriving-in-the-new-normal.

64 Bruch, H and Ghoshal, S (2002), 'Beware the busy manager', *Harvard Business Review*, hbr.org/2002/02/beware-the-busy-manager.

65 Barker, E (2019), *Barking Up the Wrong Tree: The Surprising Science Behind Why Everything You Know About Success is (Mostly) Wrong*, HarperCollins.

66 Suttie, J (2018), 'How Mind-Wandering May Be Good For You', *Greater Good*, greatergood.berkeley.edu/article/item/how_mind_wandering_may_be_good_for_you.

67 Kondo, M (2014), *The Life-Changing Magic of Tidying Up: The Japanese Art of Decluttering and Organizing*, Ten Speed Press; Kondo, M (2016), *Spark Joy: An Illustrated Master Class on the Art of Organizing and Tidying Up*, Ten Speed Press.

68 Gordon, A (2016), 'You Say VUCA, I Say TUNA: How Oxford Helps Leaders Face the Complex And Uncertain Future', *Forbes*, forbes.com/sites/adamgordon/2016/04/06/oxford/?sh=5d3f95674314.

69 Harvey, V and De Meuse, K (2021), *The Age of Agility: Building Learning Agile Leaders and Organizations*, Oxford University Press.

70 Kahneman, D (2011), *Thinking, Fast and Slow*, Farrar, Straus and Giroux.

71 Ryan, M (2020), *Michael Ryan (WHO Health Emergencies Programme) at daily press briefing on COVID 19 March 13th 2020* [video], YouTube, youtube.com/watch?v=AqRHH6e-y6I.

72 Powell, CL and Persico, JE (2003), *My American Journey*, Penguin Random House.

73 Ries, E (2011), *The Lean Startup: How Constant Innovation Creates Radically Successful Businesses*, Penguin.

74 Wade, M, Tarling, A and Neubauer, R (2017), op. cit.

75 Simpson, J (1998), *Touching the Void*, Random House.

76  Price, C (2021), *The Power of Fun: How to Feel Alive Again,* Dial Press.

77  Maslow, AH (1968), *Toward a Psychology of Being,* Van Nostrand.

78  Price, C (2021), op. cit.

79  Baird, J (2020), *Phosphorescence: On Awe, Wonder and Things That Sustain You When The World Goes Dark,* HarperCollins.

80  Mohrman, S (2007), 'Having Relevance and Impact: The Benefits of Integrating the Perspectives of Design Science and Organizational Development', Center for Effective Organizations, ceo.usc.edu/2007/03/04/having-relevance-and-impact-the-benefits-of-integrating-the-perspectives-of-design-science-and-organizational-development.

81  Duffy, J (2019), 'The Power of Perspective Taking: How leaning in can expand our worldview and deepen our relationships', *Psychology Today,* psychologytoday.com/au/blog/the-power-personal-narrative/201906/the-power-perspective-taking.

82  Haskell, R (2017), 'The Most Sought-After Architect in the World Prepares to Make His Mark on New York City's Skyline', *Vogue,* vogue.com/article/Bjarke-ingels-group-danish-architect-big.

83  Delahunty, E (2018), 'Singapore airport unveils stunning media installation', RealCommercial.com.au, realcommercial.com.au/news/Singapore-airport-unveils-stunning-media-installation.

84  Frankl, V (1959), *Man's Search for Meaning,* Beacon Press.

85  Morieux, Y (2014), *As Work Gets More Complex, 6 Rules to Simplify* [video], TED, ted.com/talks/yves_morieux_as_work_gets_more_complex_6_rules_to_simplify?language=en.

86  Suttie, J (2017), 'Four Ways Social Support Makes You More Resilient', *Greater Good,* greatergood.berkeley.edu/article/item/four_ways_social_support_makes_you_more_resilient.

87  Bullivant, S (2018), *Europe's Young Adults and Religion,* St Mary's University, stmarys.ac.uk/research/centres/benedict-xvi/docs/2018-mar-europe-young-people-report-eng.pdf.

88  Miller, L (2022), *The Awakened Brain,* Penguin Books.

89 Loehr, J and Schwartz, T (2001), 'The Making of a Corporate Athlete', *Harvard Business Review*, hbr.org/2001/01/the-making-of-a-corporate-athlete.

90 ibid.

91 International Encyclopedia of the Social Sciences (n.d.), 'Rituals', encyclopedia.com/social-sciences/applied-and-social-sciences-magazines/rituals.